T0147111

9 WORD RETHINK TO GET ON WITH LIFE

Maria Henneberry

BALBOA.
PRESS
A DIVISION OF HAY HOUSE

Copyright © 2018 Maria Henneberry.

All rights reserved. No part of this book may be used or reproduced by any means, graphic, electronic, or mechanical, including photocopying, recording, taping or by any information storage retrieval system without the written permission of the author except in the case of brief quotations embodied in critical articles and reviews.

Balboa Press books may be ordered through booksellers or by contacting:

Balboa Press
A Division of Hay House
1663 Liberty Drive
Bloomington, IN 47403
www.balboapress.com
1 (877) 407-4847

Because of the dynamic nature of the Internet, any web addresses or links contained in this book may have changed since publication and may no longer be valid. The views expressed in this work are solely those of the author and do not necessarily reflect the views of the publisher, and the publisher hereby disclaims any responsibility for them.

The author of this book does not dispense medical advice or prescribe the use of any technique as a form of treatment for physical, emotional, or medical problems without the advice of a physician, either directly or indirectly. The intent of the author is only to offer information of a general nature to help you in your quest for emotional and spiritual well-being. In the event you use any of the information in this book for yourself, which is your constitutional right, the author and the publisher assume no responsibility for your actions.

Any people depicted in stock imagery provided by Getty Images are models, and such images are being used for illustrative purposes only. Certain stock imagery © Getty Images.

Print information available on the last page.

ISBN: 978-1-9822-1577-4 (sc)
ISBN: 978-1-9822-1579-8 (hc)
ISBN: 978-1-9822-1578-1 (e)

Library of Congress Control Number: 2018913325

Balboa Press rev. date: 11/08/2018

CONTENTS

To Lucy and Liam-

May this book help you make sense of life's challenges. I love you both more than all of those infinite trips to the moon and back we used to giggle about together.

Throughout life, honor your true north. Feel deeply, think clearly, accept nothing less than kindness and decency, give kindness away with wild abandon, always stand back up, and have fun out there.

You are my singing birds.

Keep a green tree in your heart and perhaps a singing bird will come. -Chinese Proverb

WORDS

To observe or absorb is the question

WORDS MATTER

I was talking to a girlfriend about the power of words when she nodded wistfully, "This is so true, Maria. I'm triggered by the words easy and lazy when I hear them." Something causes her to flag those words based on her history. We've known each other for most of our lives and those words have no specific connection to my thoughts about her. However, she has to mentally walk herself back to center when tossed off course hearing them in reference to herself, so she doesn't carry residue from however they were hurtfully tossed at her in the past. Many of us have words like that we associate with our own pain. We can get stuck on them, consciously or unconsciously, if we don't transform how and whether we absorb them.

Words can change lives when strung together just right as

subjects, verbs, and objects to convey information. Finding the right ones to express a feeling is a significant part of process.

Words are weapons, but also medicine. They divide and unite human beings. Together, we don't give it much thought. They're easy to take for granted. Say what you have to say and move on. Words are our most heavily travelled road between each other. We hold them responsible for many trials and triumphs we face when we say something like, "Did you hear what he just said to me?!" Yet, we can do virtually nothing to control how someone uses them in our presence. Words are walls and walkways between each of us. Some people use big ones to distance attempting to self-protect and prove superiority. Others do everything they can to make sure words break through walls that separate us.

Each time we use them, we communicate who we are. We get used to certain ideas about what each one means to us. We understand there are immovable definitions. We understand people receive what we say or write based on those definitions, but even at that, we know plenty of things can impact how they're received altering what they mean such as: tone of voice, eye contact, and even silence.

There are moments one measly word made the difference to the good or bad baggage you carry from your history. Some of the best memories include word use creditable to one solitary, well-placed one. Power jockeying can mean using words with loaded meaning. Relationships can fizzle when an attempt to find the right word falls flat in a less than adequate attempt to relay a feeling.

I've conducted thousands of individual interviews throughout my digital media writing career, most of them in audio and video. It involved studying those interviews to isolate specific soundbites when someone expressed who they are, how they feel, and what they want as invisible arrows pointed toward revealing pieces of how they exist in the world.

Even if someone cannot find the right words, the feeling doesn't go away. It's still there without exception. Frankly, it's remarkable so many words and definitions stand after so many years, because our experiences change so drastically as human beings with the decades. Sitting in my favorite chair typing this book on my computer evokes some kind of feeling that someone writing a book with a quill pen and jar of ink might have felt 150 years ago, despite the fact we are handling the process so differently. Nonetheless, the feelings stand with nuanced shifts based on geography, age, topic, and any number of other factors that constantly change around us. How I think of writing a book is just a bit different than that author would have viewed writing a book 150 years ago based on technology alone. We use the same words to explain what is happening, but how we think about what those words mean is not the same. Thousands of new words pop up every year, but we have go-to mainstays that represent ideas we consider foundational in creating a framework of how we define our existence.

SPREAD THE WORD

I grew up in a family of professional entertainers as the fifth of six kids in a creative artistic traveling troupe along with our mom and dad. There was a 20-year age span from the oldest to youngest kid. My dad, Lee, was a creative leader and served as our performance ringmaster, so to speak. He ran the show as a magician and juggler. My mom, Rita, was the emotional support system for everyone and dad's support on stage. Plus, she was wildly creative making all of the costumes and equipment covers and anything else that needed our name stitched on it. She was a gifted seamstress and I'd watch her hands stitching each letter of our last name onto various pieces of cloth as she painstakingly made sure it was all evenly cut and sewn in straight lines on the velvet, canvas, and basic cotton fabrics that made up the playful, yet wildly serious lifestyle that was our world. Each of my brothers and sisters were musicians and unicyclists coming together as a family variety show traveling all over the United States and Canada. Our regimented daily practice schedule was the baseline rhythm of our lives tucked in-between school, homework, birthday parties, running around the neighborhood playing with friends, and extended family functions.

My own personal practice schedule included an hour of unicycle, an hour of gymnastics, a half hour of keyboard, a half hour of drums, and 15-20 minutes of trumpet most every day starting from the various ages I was introduced to each new skill. No matter what we practiced, we always had to end on a 'good one' of whatever stunt or piece of music we diligently worked to master on any given day. Ending on a 'good one' is a habit that carries over for me even today.

My parents took twice a year treks all over the world in their retirement years with other entertainers similar to themselves performing table and stage magic in locations from throughout Europe to Indonesia and Malaysia. They were eager travelers for a good 15 years in their retirement together.

I listened to words my dad used on stage every time we did a show. Sitting on some tucked away ledge along the side stage watching my dad's sequin and gem covered stage lit profile with microphone in hand, I'd try not to touch the velvet curtains fearing I'd reveal what was supposed to be my mouse-like presence. I was fascinated by the way his inflection could impact the crowd, the words he said, the way he changed them from show to show, and the way he moved in tandem with the specific words he chose to capture and, hopefully, mesmerize an audience. Backstage, I listened intently memorizing the old and new routines. I started to understand word rhythms and pacing he used conveying jokes, sharing anecdotes, making observations attempting to lift up that crowd with his words.

As a little girl, my younger sister, Michelle, struggled with words as she set out on her brave trek as little ones do to learn language. Nearly two years older, I became her mouthpiece answering questions others asked on her behalf. Her toddler language was mine to interpret so others could understand what she was saying. The bridge between her ability to be understood and get what she needed relied on me dutifully translating her language.

LIVING BEYOND DEFINITIONS

Who challenges well-worn definitions? There's a mathematical certainty in our assumptions about word definitions. The dictionary is it's own kind of bible.

When we hear the word power, we understand what power means to us. Despite the fact we know there are different kinds of power, we have a well-worn path to what we perceive power is based on what is probably the first definition we ever learned in grade school. Does that serve you now? That's the big picture question. A child's eye sees black and white easily. With more life experience, there are more possibilities beyond those first understandings to see a word in a broader way that serves our spirit more usefully and, hopefully, generously.

Often we believe much of what other people tell us we are versus deciding who and what we are to ourselves. Without outside support, useless assumptions can impede our healing after adversity.

Having done many interviews with people in their most triumphant and trial-laden times, it's fascinating to watch them reconcile the meaning of their experiences through deliberately chosen words that cement certainty in the framework built around their existence.

When someone stands in front of you vulnerable, hurting, embarrassed by their predicament, who will you be? Our words often tell that story. Our pain is in the words we speak to others. Our comfort, our joy, and our love of self is contained in what we send out. How it is received is where the contamination can seep in and mess with healing.

We're challenged to take hold of spoken words in a way that serves our future. I found it easy over the years to stockpile and absorb the hurt in words others used expressing personal views in snarky or dismissive ways. I didn't like how I was allowing residue of someone else's poor experiences to impact me. Consider ways to rethink some of the most well-worn words, so you can get on with life feeling renewed and ready for your new phase.

WORDS AS ART

Jewelry pendants are one of my favorite types of art to make, because they represent entire experiences in just a few words, images, and designs on small pieces of metal that fit easily in the palm of your hand. Creative hobbies are a vital outlet for me having briefly been an art minor in college, growing up with an art teacher father, receiving ribbons for my artwork along the way, and having also sold pieces in various places. My interest in art virtually always involves words. Whether painting a mural in a school cafeteria, weaving them into art, planning them out on a poster, or relying on them to convey meaning in lyrics I write, words are a cornerstone.

Books play a huge role in my jewelry pendant art projects. I enjoy hunting for the perfect word or play on words to open up new interpretations of an idea. For example, making a bookmark out of a bent-over flattened spoon with the silver handle sitting neatly between pages while the spoon itself colorfully sticks out sporting words such as 'leave a message' or 'he had been beautiful'. What does it mean out of context from it's own book pages? You decide. That's freedom.

Nobody rethinks words we take for granted. Anger is anger. Power is power. Worth is worth. But, is that true? It that true for you? A cookie-cutter did not create your experience. You are an individual with certain experiences you don't even talk about with others, because it doesn't fall in line with the status quo. They don't fall in line with everybody else. You already do the very thing this book is about in your silence. In those moments, there's an excellent chance you don't see your experience as fitting inside the lines and don't share your thoughts every single time you have them. You don't take it on, because you self-edit to keep unnecessary emotional contamination others might want to share at bay. It's common.

As a digital media producer, I've conducted interviews about extraordinary circumstances people have been through such as seeing a plane go down in the field and stopping the car to run and help. A bystander might have saved someone from drowning. Another person might have watched someone collapse stepping in to conduct CPR, offer comfort, and get involved. It's common for people in these situations to struggle for the right words to explain how they felt, the way it continues to impact them, their feeling about the person they saved, and so on.

I'm used to describing such people as heroes going above and beyond to aid someone in dire need. However, these people of all ages and backgrounds generally don't consider themselves heroes refusing to accept the label, despite the fact they live the definition. When they refer to personal experiences, hero is not their choice. They consider themselves average citizens not doing anything anyone else wouldn't have done. They say they were only doing what had to be done. They say they treated others as they would hope to be treated if the tables were turned. The idea the word hero is one they don't want to be associated with makes a point about this book. Just because the word hero expresses who they are to the public, they want no part of it. Does that make them any less a hero? Who decides?

This is an example of rethinking words. Dozens of people I've talked to in hero interviews re-define what they've done to align more with who they see themselves as not taking anything away from others who'd claim the title or use it to describe them in their own conversations. Bingo.

PEACEFUL, CONTENT & HAPPY

I've made peace with my own tough experiences throughout the years and live in a grounded contentment made of gratitude for the goodness around me. I've shared a wonderful life with people I cherish in the different phases growing and learning hands you. I'm profoundly aware of the preciousness of what surrounds me. That doesn't negate the difficulty of coping with pain.

When you live a life determined to face fears and explore new possibilities, you'll hit walls. However, while trying to climb those walls, I struggled to find people, books, counselors or anything to merely be a quiet beacon of hope for this better life I knew I could reach if I stayed my course at these various times. When I did find that, I cherished it.

Plus, it's important to note no one owns painful experiences. There is no worthiness measuring stick as to why yours is upsetting and discombobulating for you while I ought to minimize and get over mine already. The people we think cause us pain are in their own kind. Each of us make choices based on our own rocky paths and sometimes those collide. Compassion is our dearest friend on the journey even if we choose to distance from those who feel emotionally unsafe to us.

Lesson number one might be to notice if that is a contaminating idea you carry with you. Do you view some pain as less worthy than other pain? I urge you to find a way to let it go. I've learned over the years through my own trials and in interviewing, listening, and helping others that pain is pain. There is no pecking order for it. Hopefully, the pages of this book will help.

Here's what I wanted working through my own experiences with various kinds of adversity:

1- I wanted thoughts to help on an off-kilter day when someone said something unexpectedly that stung my heart or I was struggling to keep gremlins at bay in my mind. I wasn't looking for government stats in those times that I could locate on the internet.

2- I wanted to know I was loved through the reassurance of someone else sometimes when I was sick of trying to figure out how this whole self-care, self-soothing racket worked. I didn't want brutal unhelpful anonymous comments on some anonymous blog where many try to distance from their pain.

3- I wanted to hear the voice of a friend in my head and read words from their experiences that could take my hand and show me a way through, at least, some of the darkness from an entirely different vantage point, because I didn't know if I'd make it for too many days and weeks at a time. That is, until by holding on one more minute, somehow the light would start to shine one tiny beam at a time.

Ultimately? I wanted connection with someone who'd been there.

WORDS OF WISDOM

One of the most fascinating people I ever met was a simple man in his 90's with bright smiling eyes and a sweet unassuming nature. His name was Ruby and, at his advanced aged, he was still caning chairs in his small town garage to continue to be useful and make a living. I felt the love for his craft in his attitude, the way his bent brown fingers moved tenderly against the chairs he caned, and his gentle humble way. People who live life on their own terms with kind eyes and caring hearts in decency and with humility seeking to understand those around them inspire me. There are plenty of us out there sharing the journey to lift each other up not merely prove we checked off all the boxes of the American dream and 'made it' which, since you are here on this planet reading this, you have in some sense already. Our lives can have more meaning than building up a fortress of shallow success markers as forms of self-protection.

As a journalist, people often ask about interviews you enjoy most assuming you'll talk about well-known celebrities and politicians. My answer was usually a surprise because, despite having covered many well-known names, it's day to day people that inspire me. They're the ones plodding through life often without the frills and privilege of wealth and power. They live creatively, mindfully, and hopefully no matter what they've endured without Public Relations teams to mask and spin troubles or tech experts scrubbing the internet clean of their foibles. These people might not even use the internet. They look for internal validation, not external applause on the hunch, if nothing else, they're worthy of self-acceptance.

There's no shortage of famous people willing to tell you how personal success works. The thing is not everyone aspires to Hollywood fame. Many of us define success as living in contentment at peace with ourselves as our goal. We want a few strong friendships, respectful dynamics in relationships we choose, meaningful work, a healthy dose of adventure, laughter, and we don't consider name dropping or flaunting financial success as an enlightened existence signaling unapologetic self-esteem.

People all over live kind, thoughtful lives, learning lessons, yearning to connect, and define a highly successful life as much less pomp and circumstance, extravagance, and acquisition than big business, big media, and big names would bother promoting.

This journey through adversity life hands us can be hell and this journey can be extraordinary. The walk through silent suffering is bittersweet. It takes resolve. It takes courage. It takes heart - a big one, but not to take care of everyone else as you navigate adversity. The heart this takes is an energy of your spirit. If you find that energy, you'll do fine in all of the imperfect responses and reactions. You'll have them. You're human.

Your journey matters and your experience means something, no matter how simply you view your contribution. Your job is to find meaning in this pain, but there's no hurry and let no one tell you differently. In that meaning lies your power to take on the future. One of the worst, hard to understand and explain, parts of the blows of life little discussed through disappointment, adversity, and betrayals is that your future is often gone, at least the one you knew. It's as if your life gets hurled off a high cliff and you are in free fall.

For instance, it was surprising to me how unconsciously I accepted the reality of my future with my family when my father died or marriage dissolved or a job ended, even. Your fears of the futility of it all can melt away once you either make peace with this new ambiguity or identify new goals for your new future to give life the kind of meaning virtually all of us yearn for to make sense of our presence on this planet. It's weighty. It's big. It's mind-blowing. It's real.

I'm proud of you for loving yourself enough to know you can find peace and contentment if you can find the right inner tools, seek the right assistance, use your sense of adventure, creativity, and spontaneity to your own benefit by being curious about what's next; stepping into your future with kindness and openness to new experiences.

This book will help you rethink meaning out of a list of terms I found myself pummeled by in the collective dialogue. It slowed down my healing in how they're often used when compared to how I chose to see them in my on-going life quest to maintain my free-spirited can-do resilience, rational requirement that life make sense, and constant eye on personal growth.

This book is about learning a new way to love yourself.

ANGER

Anger is vulnerability repellent.

ANGER SCARES US

Anger in practice is one of the most frightening words in the English language. It's one of the primary surefire scream-provoking insurance policies in haunted houses. Dress in ripped up clothes, turn out the lights, and act very angry. Voila. Screams and terror.

Have you ever known someone or maybe it's you who makes it a point to let someone know they weren't angry with whatever happened. We seem comfortable with most any other emotion, but don't dare think the person was ever angry. Anger has a way of leaving people uncomfortable in sometimes bad and sometimes good ways. If a person gets angry, they're either at risk of losing credibility or are well-positioned to build it depending on the audience. Anger tends to be polarizing depending on how we learned to view it's impact.

Instead of being heard, the angry person will become the subject of workarounds as others attempt to navigate the anger instead of being directly with it and the person displaying it. Being with an angry person is hard. Classically, it's not lauded as a pleasant experience.

We can debate gender differences in how anger is received and I do believe there's legitimacy to a higher tolerance for male anger over female anger, but overall that growth task for anyone is to look at what it covers no matter who is using it as a tool or coping mechanism. Anger can result in a person seeming unhinged. It's not uncommon to be perceived as emotionally unstable when angry instead of merely the best idea a kind, sensitive person had in the moment to make sense of pain.

ANGER IS A PROTECTANT

More than once I've asked an angry parent in a store how they were doing and if I could help when they were lashing out at their child at a concerning level. While observing, I could tell the parent and the young child were each trying to be heard in the moment and the mutual frustration was clear with a child acting out in the presence of a tired and exasperated mom. All three of those times the mother looked at me and became emotional, as in sad, because she was struggling and needed compassion in the moment for herself as much as for her child. Why wouldn't a person such as me, a bystander shopping nearby, kindly be willing to stop for a one moment and just say, "Hi. I've been where you are and I know how hard this is sometimes. How can I help you right now?" Why would that ever be more meddlesome and less constructive than taking pictures or video from afar, turning them in to authorities, or shaming them on social media?

We seem to view anger as something to use as gotcha moments too often in public to too few useful ends. There are always cases where it's plenty useful and those become the derailing 'whataboutisms' that keep the collective dialogue distracted debating individual cases. But, as a whole, why is it we eagerly jump to anger first instead of compassion when we do have an ability to assume best intent for at least a few minutes in seeing each other as the human beings we are. What could a kind compassionate word diffuse if it is our first instinct instead of our self-protective anger?

When I see those moments amplified on social media, I wonder why the question isn't turned on the person gathering the footage more often to ask, "What kept you from asking how you could be of service versus using your phone camera as a social bullying tool to get someone to step back in line with what you deem as socially appropriate behavior?" Sure, there are definitely times the behavior needs to be addressed differently and with more involvement from authorities. However, in all three cases I've experienced in public, the parent looked at me and cried. Just the pause, kind word, and gentle clue-in changed that parent child dynamic. Compassion without judgment shifted the energy in a constructive way. Why is anger something to be afraid of unless it's because we are afraid of our own?

There's a good chance you've known someone in your life who is a zero to anger person not stopping at many, if any, emotions along the way. When you're surrounded by people who live a zero to anger life, it's not hard to find someone else near them compensating by numbing, becoming more pleasant, or walking on eggshells. That balancing dynamic works like peanut butter and jelly smashed together between two pieces of fresh bread. There are others who join in with the angry people and help them lead the charge fueled by mutual fear. Still, there are others who cruelly enjoy manipulating moments to provoke angry reactions satisfying a warped desire to control others.

Anger doesn't make you bad. It makes you human. It's sadness on steroids. Anger is the best idea some people have in the moment to distance, say their peace, express their pain, find their voice, feel safe even if it's ineffective. Even though we hear being kind is the way to go, being kind doesn't mean you're never angry. That kindness extends to you, too. Be kind to yourself by paying attention to what does anger you, so you can address what it covers.

DEGREES OF ANGER

I've gone through a few phases in regard to anger. Difficult decisions I've made throughout life demonstrate that I will stand ground and some of those moments are peppered throughout this book. Many challenging choices from teenage years till now show I look life directly in the eyes to make hard decisions on my own behalf and on behalf of my children, not worried about rocking the boats of others when safety is in question. Plus, I have to stand up for myself. It's how I'm made. People pleasing doesn't feel good to me. It feels like a lie. A flexible adaptable human being? Definitely. But, even that is not without curbs. When I do hurt people in situations involving a hard decision on my own behalf, it is generally tough and part of life's process of learning and growing. One of the best compliments I have ever received was when an old childhood friend told me he knows I'm a 'what you see is what you get' kind of person. Being told you're authentic is a huge compliment.

That said, it took some years to rid myself of the 'good girl' cloak championed throughout my school career as I headed into adulthood. As a 'good girl', I didn't bother getting very angry growing up. It didn't fit the template I had of myself at home, with friends, or in school, so I didn't let it happen. Interestingly, I was smart enough to avoid it mostly because I had a decent understanding of people. I could pretty much anticipate moments that left me angry before they even happened, so I made it my job to develop workarounds. I didn't blow off handing in assignments that would result in anger. I didn't wait to be asked 20 times to get something done at work turning someone around me and myself into anger smokestacks. It didn't seem difficult and the pay off was great. Keep your word, do what you promise to do, keep things on the up and up and it'll work out. I was more likely to be kindly assertive than passive, by nature. It kept my good girl status intact.

In college, I started to have strange little fits of anger once in a while. My parents came to the university to bring me a rolling globe which is a gigantic hard ball you walk on. As a member of a collegiate circus, this was one of my acts. My father and I were switching the ball from their car to mine in an Italian restaurant parking lot and a group of kids decked out in all-black clothing walked by and heckled me with my gigantic ball. OK, I knew it was an unusual sight as a big-haired college female rolling her huge white ball through a campus restaurant parking lot. I was a bit of a sitting duck for ridicule. Deep down, I knew I was an amusing image, but I was having none of it that day standing there with my father and my giant ball. I lit into the goth students angry that, in their counter culture state, were actually making fun of me for not looking mainstream in that moment. The irony made me angry.

My dad was stunned by my willingness to snap back at total strangers exchanging words in that parking lot. He turned to me and said, "Don't worry about them. Keep your eyes on your own business. They aren't your concern." But, in that moment they were. They represented too many frustrating things about the world to me: bullying, hypocrisy, groupthink, and lack of sincere humble curiosity. If they had been taking on my gender, too, I

17

might have blown more than one gasket. I would not allow myself to be a victim and that's how it played out with me in that state of mind at age 20. I fought back.

My dad was silent with me after that and I could tell he understood my anger having been challenged with his own brand over the years. He didn't mention it to my mom or anyone else. I could tell he saw me differently after that which was good as the good girl chains continued to fall away. I had to shake them off somehow.

Another moment of anger related to my collegiate circus days riding my unicycle between the practice gym and my dormitory. I was in a university with one of the only student circuses in the country and it was an eclectic group of wildly talented students. I could have carried my unicycle home that particular night, but it made no sense when I had one to ride. That said, unicycles aren't the best option for getting anywhere fast. The classic design barely moves at a speed faster than a brisk walk, but is better exercise because of all the muscle work.

As I rode my unicycle by a neighboring dormitory on this cool spring evening, I heard a guy heckle me from high above my head out of one of the windows of the dormitory next to mine. He didn't stop. This is how invincible an angry college student disillusioned by gender inequity can be when sprayed with words intolerant of anything that isn't celebrating all that is homogenous.

I stepped off my unicycle in the dark of the night, with street lights shining down on the two of us in all directions. I lifted my unicycle with one arm and I held my other fist in the air calling out to the wall of nameless windows, "You think you are so tough yelling at me from some anonymous dorm room? Come down here and tell that to me to my face! I'm not afraid of you!" And, I waited. I gently set my unicycle down next to me and patiently stood next to it all by ourselves, my one-wheeler and me. Nothing happened. That 30-second thrill by some no name guy in one of hundreds of windows on a university campus of thousands meant nothing and it was everything to me in my anger in that moment. I hopped back on my unicycle and continued riding to my room. I never forgot either instance because I was surprised by my own fierce resolve in each moment. I was justice-oriented and had such an eye on human dignity as a right for all, that in each of those moments feeling vulnerable - one that I'd be ridiculed in front of my dad who along with my mom had done something kind for me by bringing to school that globe in a special trip and the other when I felt vulnerable as a young woman alone at night on a college campus doing my own thing - I could no longer bend. I broke. My 'good girl' cloak was cracking. I was starting to demand more space and elbow room for my depth and knowledge of my worthiness to hold ground for myself.

As I moved into my 20's, that 'good girl' game was no longer useful. I understood it made life more comfortable for some other people, but I was coming into my voice and the voice didn't always have a popular view. Plus, I'd gone through more anger provoking moments, many of which were control and gender-related. As a result, I wore anger with righteousness and, ultimately, a bit of melancholy. Enter musicians that sang the songs I'd have liked to sing myself such as Alanis Morissette, Ani DiFranco, Tori Amos, Sarah McLachlan, Shawn Colvin, and the Indigo Girls.

My family wasn't entirely sure what to do with my brand of anger. But, I needed a way to own my voice with more relevance for my life. I was a good kid - a good girl - who wanted the best for others and was tired of being mistreated because I looked like some kind of good girl target. I had absorbed sexual harassment multiple times already and had been violated by someone I had only met the same night he raped me, to name two specific reasons I created my musical sisterhood of cds. I share more of these experiences in later chapters Power and Worth. It helped me see me the way I was, not the way anyone outside of me wanted me to be. I was proud of my anger in that time, because it fueled my fire keeping me alert and safe. I was ready for whatever could be thrown at me. I would have my own back and the back of anyone around me, because I could protect myself and what I cared about now.

CONSUMED WITH ANGER

During this time, one of the side effects of not knowing how to hold space in the world was funky eating patterns. I was nursing an eating disorder. I was flipping back and forth from eating nothing for a few days at a time to periods I'd purge when I felt overwhelmed. It was hardly unusual in the circles of young women around me. Plus, at the time, the widespread disordered eating pattern known affectionately as 'drive-thru order by number' was being culturally championed as saving busy people time and money promoted as wise, efficient decision-making. In addition, there were more than a couple candy bar vegetarians in my social network. I was hardly surrounded by thoughtful food consumption, so what I was doing didn't seem like that big of a deal - for a while.

The social conversation about the prevalence of eating disorders was gaining momentum and I knew I had some version of that, but wasn't sure what to name it because it swung from militantly healthful eating all the way to no eating. I would be fine for a while and then I'd hit rough patches where I'd slip into the behaviors again. I heard some media interviews about the connection between eating disorders and not feeling pretty enough, so I tried to look for that connection in my own struggle. But, the looks and beauty perspective did not connect dots for me. I was ashamed of my misdirected coping strategy initially sparked as an experiment in high school after seeing a Primetime Live report by Diane Sawyer on the subject. I was curious. Maybe it was a subconscious rebellion even that first time. I have no way of being certain.

After that first time of tiptoeing into disordered eating patterns, I didn't do it again for years until one day feeling like I was going to burst in college with a need to control something in my own life, I used it as a way to deal in the moment and a troubling behavior began. I understood with time as I paid close attention to what triggered my desire to slip into eating disordered behavior was that it took hold of me when I didn't feel my voice was valued. It helped me cope. If my voice wasn't welcome, something else would come out of my mouth or wouldn't be allowed in at all.

As a good girl who thought and felt deeply, it became a way to balance out the injustices of the title with the real, textured me underneath. It was a form of anger growing alongside my maturing advocacy-oriented articulate voice in surroundings that didn't know what to do with that kind of young female besides pat her on the head and send her on her way. With our unusual upbringing, my family taught me to have an independent female voice and I was now trying to find a place to put it.

Channeling anger toward good was key to my accomplishing much in my professional life. My career and volunteerism took off, because I needed a place to put well-meaning anger to feel good about the outcome. But, it burned out when I was less underdog and more personal success story having worked hard in those years. My benevolent anger no longer fit. I looked inside and began to see the fear, sadness, disappointment, and insecurity anger covered for me. I began to address that.

As for how I channeled my eating disordered behavior to

quell the anger, I sought help. With my older sister, Mary Zita's guidance, I found an eating disorder counselor and talked with her. I found myself in a support group with other young women with disorders alarmed and touched by their struggles and difficulties. I was skimming the surface by comparison realizing I was still able to be in a place of observing and studying my behavior. It hadn't pulled me all the way under yet. It came and it went for a few years until I owned the place I stood and began to respect the strength of my voice.

I found a solution that worked for me and I offer it in the interest of sharing my story, but I don't recommend it as a solution for anyone. If it is helpful, that's awesome. But, I don't have any way to fully understand the scientific reasons my approach made the difference for me. I credit my solution working for me to my seeking nature, relentless willingness to absorb and learn, and a decision to find something that could work. I had to want the solution more than I wanted the behavior which is much too simplistic for most people coping with disordered eating behavior which I, make no mistake, fully respect and understand.

I could tell my disordered eating behavior was becoming a way to have a ritual for myself that was just for me and gave me a sense of useful control over my own destiny as I saw it. I needed to replace it to change it. So, my effort at a solution was to became vegetarian. The reason this helped me is it gave me an advocacy that was bigger than me which was an ideal approach for a giving young woman. It had a spiritual aspect to it, as in there was respect for other life forms around us in my considering my food intake each day which was also bigger than me. It was a kind of self-care that required no excuse or apology even when asked why I'd eat that way. It created instant, easy to name, curbs and a sense of control in a chaotic world. Plus, it was a more creative way to see and consume food than what was surrounding me at that time which reached me as a creatively-minded person. I was vegetarian for nine years until my first child was born and by then, in my particular case, disordered eating behavior was long behind me. It was no longer useful to me. I found that awareness interesting and telling about the voice we don't always champion in kids when we peg them as 'good girls' and 'good boys.'

What triggers my anger now is watching someone be disrespected and disregarded as in any type of bullying. I sometimes feel anger swell inside of me on behalf of the person being hurt or myself. Mix that with lies my intuition flags when people attempt to manipulate me and voila.

What do I do when angry? Immediately jumping to what sadness, insecurity, or fear my anger is covering in me at that moment is my well-worn part now. I address that. I don't get rip roarin' mad very often because it's not my nature to do that as I've shared, plus I've done so much internal work over the years, it's become less useful to me on my path.

As a mom, when I do have an occasional angry moment such as with one of my kids I sit with them and talk through whatever my trigger might have been in the moment. I'm fully aware the anger would be about my stuff, not theirs. I own it, because I want them to see my imperfection. It's my best idea for helping lead them to a place of peace with their own foibles as they grow up. I don't want them to feel an ounce of shame about a moment I showed anger. While I don't have control over their reaction, I can assume responsibility for my part in it. My hope is that example benefits them as adults. My goal is to teach my children not what to think, but how to think. One of the ways that happens is for them to see my humanness.

Rethink Challenge: The goal with anger is to use it as a personal alarm. When it goes off, look inside. Anger covers sadness and fear when we look closer. The question becomes

what sadness and fear is your angry moment covering? Anger is such a great tool for building self-awareness. Use your angry moments to your own advantage by addressing what triggers it, so it doesn't have a leg to stand on anymore in your thoughts.

BEAUTY

Until your beauty is on your terms, others control you.

PUBERTY IS NO PARTY

I've been aware of my body and the fact it had a mind of its own since I hit puberty. I got my period at age 12 and five months, December 29th at 10:30a while watching The Love Boat on the living room TV with my siblings, Mark and Michelle. I was so mad, sad, scared, and out of sorts when it happened, I went numb that day waiting for my mom to get home from a shopping trip so I could ask her to come into the bathroom and talk about what happened as if my body and I were in a fight. I wanted her to take my side. It was a teary, embarrassing, scary experience to become a woman.

It didn't matter that my mom was standing in front of me having dutifully had a comprehensive sex talk years before now telling me about the beautiful blossoming that was happening.

25

That sex talk had happened in my parent's bedroom when I was nine-years-old after coming home from school and asking what the f-word meant which I'd heard boys saying to each other on the playground. My mom sat me down shortly after telling me she would've preferred putting off the talk another year or so, but felt it was important now after my questions. Our discussion included a vintage two-foot tall Visible Woman model with the bonus Miracle of Creation plastic parts mom pulled from a box. She laid it out on my parent's bed showing me how babies grow and turn upside down while living next to internal organs for months all viewable through the plastic lady's perfect puzzle of a transparent body. She shared the vital information and left pamphlets I was encouraged to slip in and seek out at my convenience in the top drawer of her bedroom dresser along with her pledge for a 24-7 open door policy to ask questions. She'd done her part A+ well and I was still not embracing this new phase of life.

I attempted to shun this new version of me my body seemed to want to become and I was angry I had to leave behind a version of myself I liked just fine. When I first learned about sex and all that went with it, I told myself I'd hold my period like you can hold your bladder. However, periods don't care about bladder protocol and are rebels that way. Yet, I had it all figured out until I was a 12-year-old and it happened. Then, I was out of sorts. I learned I had much less command of my body than I thought and any sense of teenage entitlement I might've been nurturing began to dissipate.

Just the fact I can pinpoint the start and emotional tone of the experience so vividly says something about my comfort or discomfort with my physicality in that time. The comfort is I felt a command over it, however misguided. The discomfort shows how emotionally aware I was, funneling virtually every experience of my life through the sieve of my emotions. This whole episode was my way of clamoring for a way to keep my experience with my body on my own terms. The trouble was I had no better way to articulate it yet.

WOMEN OWN THEMSELVES

Women will turn the entire culture on its head once we collectively learn to self-validate and not look to others for approval of our appearance or for anything about our bodies, for that matter. If we start from a place of filling ourselves on both levels, we become an authority of ourselves and then know ourselves well-enough to have something to share with others. Plus, we won't allow anyone else dominion over us. This sounds sensible, but countless examples show up every day that indicate this is not happening. In fact, our human right to personal autonomy is politicized in ways I'm stunned women and others who support us allow to happen in too many situations.

Rethinking beauty on your own terms is not about accomplishment. It's not about ego-boosting and empty words. It's about allowing ourselves to feel alone with no one to rely but ourselves for everything so we actually learn to be with ourselves entirely and enjoy it. For some women this comes more naturally than others. We are each different.

We must love being with ourselves and love what we are to be able to give to another in a way that doesn't risk our depletion. You value holding on to what makes you you when relying on yourself for what you require. What starts out one way can end in an entirely different way to the good or bad. Progress is always possible mid-journey.

I'm a woman who thought I had this figured out passionate about women's issues, our innate power, and aware of so many mind traps and day-to-day obstacles, not to mention conditioning that can make self-validation a hazy idea. I was starting out my career, educated and aware and I still found myself grappling with and at the mercy of not being able to release myself from the good girl idea which involved the currency that is external approval. I knew and still couldn't avoid all of the rabbit holes.

There's a systemic expectation in how we define beauty and we are not to a point yet where that definition stems from the woman herself. She is often a willing participate in carrying out it's contaminating damaging impact, however.

IT'S HOW I'M MADE

With a strong Irish heritage what that means for my particular body is: I'm fair-skinned, have freckles, I'm nearly hairless except for what's on my head. My eyes are sometimes equally light and dark. I like that about my eyes. They have travelled with me my whole life and are still as they have always been which is wide-eyed blue, green, and grey with golden brown flecks. They aren't hazel, blue, green, or grey. They are all of those colors. People have stopped me to comment on my eyes. They look like anyone else's from a distance, but when you look closely they're not quite the same. They reflect a bit of all possible eye colors and each one looks a little different viewing the world. There's a symbolic parallel there for me about how I live and see life.

My high forehead was first called out to me as a biological error at age nine walking home with one of the harsher, socially precocious girls from school. She asked me in a pseudo-serious tone, "So tell me, how do you get your forehead so shiny?" In my idealism, I received it as a sincere inquiry as we all want the best for each other and want to help each other along, of course. I chose to accept it as a compliment until I went home and told my mom in my happy-go-lucky 'look how nice she was to me today' tone.

Mom was cutting vegetables for dinner, slowed down her

cutting, didn't look up from what she was doing, and said to me, "Who said that, Maria?" I could feel mom's protective skepticism in her words as I watched the slowing of that knife. That was when I realized there was a word called snark and this classmate was a living, breathing definition of sinister. I was always just me bee-bopping along figuring I was ok or as my dad called me, 'a fine girl'. I didn't overthink my physicality with brutal self-talk at that stage. Insecure? Yes, that had started, but barely. Brutal self-talk? No, that was years away yet.

Indoctrination into the game of weight began in grade school and I instinctively understood health was supposed to be the goal. However, I was aware that fitting into certain sized clothing as long as possible was some worthwhile arbitrary target, too, mainly because that's all I saw people respond to socially anywhere. In the way people described women, I remember thinking they were often categorized as stunning, pretty, ok, ugly, or some kind of lost cause. Even then, I saw how society classifies females like a change sorter organizes coins. I picked up on the idea early of women being grouped by hair color and wondered why men were never talked about like that. I watched the harsh immeasurable damaging impact of it rippling through the culture around me as a young girl in grade school.

My cooking debut in the family kitchen involved inviting my best friend to make whole wheat cookies together. In my little girl logic, research told me with certainty the answer to weight control was making what you eat not buying it ready to go. Plus, my gut instinct was that the goal was to use ingredients as close to original form as possible, but that wasn't a very exciting way to think about food prep in that time.

My entire childhood and well into my 20's were marked by a regular drumbeat of news and entertainment media stories contradicting each other about what did and didn't constitute healthful eating. It was immensely confusing. Considering weight control at age nine? I had no idea I was waving a red flag already.

MY BEAUTY MY TERMS

I was practicing gymnastics an hour a day and unicycle an hour a day, mixing that with my generally active nature. It translated into tree climbing, running around the neighborhood, playing on our trampoline and the large former grade school playground set in our large lush green, meadow-like back yard. There was competitive scooter soccer in gym class, and any other way I could contort my young nimble body for my own amusement while answering my mind's call for adventure. My body did me proud and sported skills that set the trajectory of my life toward sports and activity. I was active and loved to exercise. I was comfortable with my physicality when it was on my own terms.

However, something happened along the way. I lost control of my own physical experience as others began to make my body their business. It was as if my body invaded their space in some way and they felt they had a right to issue opinion about how I held space now.

Catcalls from grown men began as a junior high girl crossing the street. My first memory of this very idea was when I was wearing my brand new baggy Lee jeans at age 13 proud of my new clothes, but ashamed when a man three times my age hollered his approval of my body across the street. I didn't understand how I was supposed to be flattered when I felt scared. I started to hear more unsolicited assessments of whether I fit cultural norms by boys and girls and adults at school and, most anywhere, frankly. I wanted to fit in at school and enjoyed wearing fashionable clothing, but wearing trendy clothes such as my snug Gloria Vanderbilt Jeans and chunky-heeled Dexter leather shoes contained a trade off. It opened the door to being judged by the collective standard. Plus, as grown men noticed me, the fun loving power I felt as a girl morphed into a fear for my safety, a fear that would continue to impact me as I got older, resulting in sexual harassment and, ultimately, rape which I talk about in later chapters. I was 12, 13, 14, 15, 16, 17. I didn't know who I was yet and wasn't actively looking for ways to sexualize my own view of myself, much less need to be molding myself to expectations, approval, or disapproval of grown men and unempowered women with one dimensional calls that I be ladylike.

If a person can assess my value outwardly and others hear and do nothing, it's social consent. Given that, what power could I have as a child? None. The messages were clear. There are people who tell themselves grown men giving attention to underage girls isn't a big deal and is merely biology. Relax and get over it. It was huge for me and I didn't understand why so many other people had trouble seeing it, too.

I have strong legs and umpteen years of unicycling and gymnastics, in addition to my heritage, who I am, and how I'm built. My legs have carried me far and I love them. I didn't always feel that way externalizing my value enough that too much of my self-worth was tied up in outward approval and trying to meet a simplistic social standard. I was swept up in the wave of 'good girl' sentiment that took hold of me conditioning me to care about what others thought. It's hard to argue with, at least for a while, when it works well for you as a teenage girl.

Considering my inherited high forehead and strong legs that were my body's way of going rogue on culture, I felt peaceful about my physicality. All of it makes me me in an age it can be hard to see and appreciate distinguishing characteristics in people that separate them from the masses in appearance. In an effort to fit in, more people all the time manipulate their bodies to be as close as possible to culturally championed ideals, whoever and whatever those ideas are, in a given year.

RUNNING FROM HERITAGE

Recently, I was attempting to describe someone to a friend to see if we both knew this person mutually. I couldn't come out with any distinguishing characteristics, because as it happens this person had manipulated themselves physically into a common homogenized form. Is that a put down? No. It's an awareness that many people manipulate their physicality away from the heritage that led them to the life they live now. How can that daily disconnection from what you sprang from not have some kind of disconnecting negative impact on a person? I have no certain answer, but it has always struck me as a useful question and it started with my own awareness. When I value my heritage in all of it's texture, I have a different kind of foundation of self-acceptance we don't talk about much, if at all. We learn and we grow and we can definitely change in a myriad of ways, but pretending the past didn't exist in how we manipulate our bodies creates interesting questions.

I remember loving my body. It was awesome. I didn't know any different. I was just me with my long stringy brown hair and my eyes peaking through a spray of bangs across my high forehead. My eyes were curious and my mind was free from the clutter of a culture that wanted to own my experience because I was a female. In my shorts and halter tops, probably worn three days in a row on my limber body, running barefoot on rocks, in sand, on dirt, and grass feeling everything under my toes, feeling everything with my ankles and my legs, feeling everything with my hands, my face, and my heart. Then one day it began to change. My body didn't feel the same anymore because the feelings I'd been learning to love were no longer appropriate in society. I was learning in classrooms and the world that I needed to temper my feelings of all kinds and I needed to control how I came across physically finding a balance between what men and women wanted and thought was appropriate. This kind of high wire act didn't do me any self-acceptance favors.

I can't exactly pinpoint the moment, but I can say this. From the middle of grade school on, it could have been mean-spirited words of a snooty girl here and a rude boy there, an unenlightened adult here and judgmental perfectionistic adult there, but it all involved words. I started to realize I apparently wasn't what I was supposed to be whatever this elusive goal was. I was so many things with so many possibilities before me as a little girl, and one road was narrowing. It was that I could physically meet any standard of beauty I was hearing about through virtually every channel in my life. It's as if a birth lottery was supposed to be the only path and I didn't have that ticket. So, I learned to be ashamed of my body.

I was modest by nature anyway running toward an authentic power for my career life one day and couldn't see how I could achieve that without fashion modesty. I had not defined beauty for myself and did not live in surroundings that championed that much independent thought in a woman either. That's despite the fact my family lived such a theatrical and cerebral life with parents who championed career equity for daughters and sons.

It sunk in when I was about 14 and a size 5. The curves were coming and I wanted nothing to do with them. I was strong from nearly a decade of daily gymnastics practices, and more than a decade of daily unicycle practicing. I was in track and a basketball player. I was muscular and life was changing my body. I was so often being reminded it was changing by those around me, boys and girls, men and women. I wanted to shun the changes in hope I could go back to the grass, the dirt, and the rocks. Nature didn't judge me and I didn't judge myself when I was in the trees, grass, and by the water. I just felt great about myself in those places.

I experienced beauty as an art project from the time I was a little girl. I would decorate my face, belly, limbs in baby powder with my little sister and run around the house in sometimes just underwear and maybe a halter top coaxing compliments from family members for our powder puff white faces that more than once ended up a mess of the fine white dust all over the floor creating a trail between several rooms.

Once at age four with my two-year-old sister in tow, I forgot I left the water on in our second floor bathroom. My older brother, Mick, in his late teens at the time, was babysitting watching Green Acres in the living room as water overflowed the sink, flooded the bathroom, made its way out of the room, and down the stairs to where my brother was lounging. When he turned around and realized what was happening, the first floor ceiling of our house was soaked with chunks of ceiling eventually falling to the floor. It was more than a few weeks job to have the ceiling replaced all because I was distracted by my pre-k beauty regimen in the bathroom and the glorious art project it was to me, already doing my part in playing my culturally dutiful role to indoctrinate my little sister into this cult of beauty.

THEATRICS OF APPEARANCE

In our traveling professional entertainment lives, we often found ourselves with time between shows. My dad might sit backstage talking to other entertainers as he folded silks presented with grandeur when pulled out of a mysterious box or reset magic illusions full of secrets. I'd hear stories and laughter echo through the empty auditoriums. My siblings might sprawl out on theater seats reading, practicing music, or might have escaped to explore our surroundings. My mom would often hang out in the dressing room repairing costumes, organizing them, or entertaining my little sister, Michelle, and me each significantly younger than the four older kids, Marg, Mary Zita, Mick, and Mark. It was not uncommon for our dressing rooms on the road to have giant theatrical vanities with wall-wide mirrors and intense bright lighting that only made my little girl draw to turn my face into an art project more rational. The art palette that was my face could turn into anything with mediums at hand: eye shadow, lipstick, eye liner and fake eyelashes out of my mom and older sisters' make up bags. My favorite toys were face powder compacts. You can have a lot of fun with a couple of mirrors.

When we performed, culture was at a turning point. Sportier clothing was coming into style. We were in the first phases of spandex and Jane Fonda's view of active fashion made the most sense at the time. I begged my parents for sportier costumes something that did not involve sequins, opera hose, and ballet slippers. It was, in part, because as a gymnast and school athlete, I was part of a generation of change moving women from less active and certainly less fashion-consciousness in that activity toward what would eventually become grounded fashionable athletic comfort for women. It was the 80's and clothing technology was a future away. At the time, cuts of clothing and something as simple as a thick headband to catch sweat were the best ideas yet and I ate it up.

Before performances, I'd dutifully put on my opera hose and sequin outfit, as my mom was a capable creative seamstress. I changed my clothes wishing for something that made me, in essence, less sparkly, shiny, and visible. Still, I wore my performance uniform like a comfortable old shoe because I was confident in my long-practiced seriously taken stage skills. My exposure to stage life had taught me to understand there's some nonsense in image as I saw how it could be constructed.

I watched countless performers magically transform their appearance from unremarkable to a magazine slick when their act began. It was nothing short of marvelous. There was exquisite art in the construction of such fantasies where stage entertainment dwells for an observant girl looking for wonder in the world. It was beautiful. The rhinestones, fabric sheens, plumes, jewels, beading, sparkles, shimmering beauty everywhere, and I was growing up in the middle of it watching with a front row seat as my own mother joined in creating beautiful costumes left and right. We had family costume sets of red, lime and dark greens, aqua, blues, purple; a rainbow of body suits and gowns all sewn together in love with a touch of fantasy by an imaginative mother for her family.

One of my favorite toy boxes on the road was a tackle box full of rhinestone jewelry in all designs, colors, and extravagance. I couldn't wait to open it at every venue, so I could dream and play with all of those tiny prisms of possibility.

That was my beauty starting point. That and knowing I wasn't to touch the wig boxes of my two older sisters, Marg and Mary Zita, nor their fake eyelashes that sat on a shelf in the RV during our traveling performances. Each box held their hair piece which glamorized their teens and 20s appearance in seconds with a few hairpins and a little spray as they fashioned their hair into a polished elegant high beehive type of updo. I watched as they used dark eye liner pencils to extend the line underneath each eye which actually made their eyelashes look even more dramatic. I longed to draw that kind of glamour on myself for fun. I saw the construction of beauty from the inside and it was a fascinating glorious view. Overall, it looked like too much work to this freedom-focused, gypsy-hearted little girl who yearned for her rocks, sky, water, and trees.

PAGEANTRY OF BEAUTY

In college, I got a phone call from a person representing my home county. Mine was one of the smallest counties in my state. It wouldn't likely take an hour to drive from county line east to west in any direction. The midwestern town I grew up in had about 1200 residents at the time and was one of only a couple good-size towns within county borders. In fact, we have a milky white old-time courthouse in the center of my hometown set back from the main street through town in a large grassy park-like setting. It's a quiet, picturesque midwestern small town with the kind of idyllic scenes people pine for in quaint independent films.

The call was about a queen contest. Our county was apparently so small there was debate about whether or not it would have one. They needed a queen to compete and do what was necessary to represent at the state beauty pageant at the state fair. I'd spent a life on stage and had no concerns about coming up with a talent. The snag for me was the fact I'd spent my entire life up to that point accomplishing things to prove my worth beyond my body to myself as much as anyone else with a long list of activities and clubs in my senior year book that meant something to me. It told me I was doing all I could to be all I could, because that's what I was taught to do. Be useful.

Many young women would have loved that phone call asking them to represent the county in a queen contest. But I said no because I was working hard to be taken seriously for my intellect and in developing skills for professional trajectory in a way I believed wasn't a phantom power that would go away with time. I let it go while watching women continue to be revered, often solely, for their appearance and wonder about the bizarre duplicity in their acceptance of the idea that they have a shelf life. It has left me wondering, at times: What was I fighting for in my decision if things haven't changed?

I've come to understand, there are many small wins on the way to big victories. Small wins happen every day. I consider my own independent decisions through my teenage and adult years some of those small wins on behalf of women. Each woman does her part in her own way and it shows in how she lives her life and lets it unfold. I don't even think I mentioned that whole queen contest episode to much of anyone. I was becoming and owning my independence.

I begged off the same kind of idea from a different vantage point again in my career about 10 years later when kindly asked to judge a queen contest in another county. It was an idea I was entirely certain was not my thing by this time.

I noticed something in my 20's watching competitive beach volleyball competitions on television as I wrestled with why I struggled for my place in this cultural pageantry of beauty. The strong-bodied bikini-clad women with all of their bump, set, spike teamwork showed extraordinary strength and a powerful grace representing a kind of femininity that gave me strength which was so much different than what I'd seen in mass media to that point. I'd been inundated by disempowering, submissive sexuality hard to escape on department and grocery store checkout magazine racks and in movie after movie and television show after television show. I got tired of the feeling I was expected to want to absorb so much sensory assaulting messaging and imagery. The key to beauty in my eyes was now clear and involved recognizing strong, powerful femininity as having it's own agency. It was less about the body itself, than the independence, strength, voice, and personal power it was about and I could finally articulate to myself the kind of beauty I valued for myself.

A few years after that, on a Mediterranean cruise with my spouse at the time, I was in a yoga class and the instructor caught my attention afterward to ask if I'd help model athletic clothes for the ship spa in a deck show for passengers. It was an effort to sell spa clothing. This time I said yes. I was on a new adventure, so what was one more that could also serve as a good test for myself? I felt more comfortable in my own skin at this stage of life having built my self-definition beyond my own high school bedroom mirror. Most importantly, this request was something I could champion; athletic workout wear for women. That spoke to who I was and it fit together in a way I felt I could honor who I was at that time.

I owned me and my image. I was no longer at a stage of life self-protecting to maintain ownership of my own body with so many people eager to own the physical experience of a women as theirs to judge, shun, envy, or lust. I owned me. I knew it in theory in my teens and I allowed that to turn into a bit of a fist in the air challenge to men who dared attempt cross the threshold as I entered my 20's, but after some years I was no longer white knuckling it through that forest of trees.

There was no concern others might take ownership of my physical experience with their opinions of my value as determined by the sum total of whatever arbitrary number showed up on a bathroom scale. I was no longer trying to keep the phantom power we call physical attractiveness at bay. I knew my value as me whether or not I was 'pleasing' enough to the 'anyone who would have me' or 'no one could possibly be good enough for me' poisons we're fed from day one as little girls in the world. As much change as we've experienced in this way culturally, we're not even close to the full shift necessary to actually change the tide in a way that doesn't have women and the daughters and sons we raise keeping the phantom at a distance. As long as beauty is allowed to be a currency of perceived value, it's an on-going battle and will polarize the population.

BRAVE BEAUTIFUL WOMEN

It's time to shift away from allowing others to define your own beauty to you. If there is any chance these words below wind with you through your days, you're likely tired of your own thinking and want new ideas. We can get used to the habit of negative self-talk and the world it builds around us can turn into a cozy blanket of predictability. If you're not careful, it can be mighty difficult to find your way out.

There's a decent chance this is a familiar dialogue you have with yourself. Note how often something positive or hopeful pops up.

I am fat.
I am powerless.
I have lost track of myself.
Less food all day.
What am I doing to myself?
I don't enjoy food I eat that much.
I feel like I can't escape food!
I get so tired of dealing with food.
I don't seem to be able to see myself clearly.
I need more exercise.
I need more water.
I need help.
I look terrible.
I am wearing pain.
Hey! I'm looking healthy today.
I've worked so hard to heal myself.
I'm feeling good!
I'm tired.
I'm discouraged.
I'm sad.

So sad.

I've taken responsibility.

I've done so much work.

I've done too much to try to be healthy and thoughtful and wise in my dealings and I'm just sad, disappointed and discouraged now.

Will the kind of change that adds positive things to my life ever come?

I don't feel good about myself anymore.

I can't seem to find my way back.

I feel like a loser and a lost cause.

I feel like a failure.

Now, go back and count how many of those reflected what you value and not what you think the external world expects of you.

You can't possibly feel your own beauty and define it for yourself if you slip into this shame spiral.

You have a responsibility to yourself to stand in the beautiful you already are loyal to yourself before allowing someone else to define it in any other way than how you want to love yourself.

These are questions of a lifetime for oodles of women and men scorched by cultural fallout of changing times, attitudes, and reverence to this phantom power built on other people's terms resulting in our money, career trajectory, and lives being caught in its web. Why do we allow our culture to give us an expiration date as women?

Why do we allow our culture to give us an expiration date as women?

41

Rethinking the word beauty is a choice, because there's always a choice in everything we do. Some might say, but I have to get a job. I have to be accepted. This is a challenge of our time. Defining beauty on your terms sets up life in a way your terms matter. You have a right to a cultural contract that benefits you, too. It's logic. Women cannot be in control of their own destiny if they're beholden to the externalization of their image on terms outside of themselves.

The focus is on women here, but it's true for men and woman alike. You cannot craft a life that keeps you in control of your own destiny when you allow others a primary voice in how you hold space in the world. The question is whether or not you are willing to fight for your own human dignity. When your appearance becomes a measuring stick for your very value as a living breathing human being, others can always control you. Some people are fine with that, but I have always known from the time I made that first whole wheat cookie in my childhood kitchen in 4th grade, living that way could never be enough for me. I was enough, but that kind of life was not and there was no way around it. My life became a quest in recognizing myself in my choices and maintaining my commitment to myself.

I paid close attention to this very idea heading into an on-camera media career. It resulted in entrepreneurial decisions that helped me rely less on whims of others and more on my ability to plan my own future, make choices to serve that future, be creative on my terms, and reduce unnecessary thought contamination by others. It makes you a wild card in the world. It's a freedom that feels wonderful.

We have a way of fixating on certain parts of ourselves, but not others. It's a curious thing. In other words, if we know we don't have control over our bodies, medically and otherwise, we aren't human beings exhibiting a full sense of agency. If I have to prove myself to someone to get something I need to live my life, I'm tossed into a measurement system, ultimately, feeling inadequate to myself, at some point. I either accept that as the only way it can be or feel rage and anger until I take full control of beauty as my own decision. Once you see it, you can decide to make difference choices, and disengage from toxic conversations by constructing an existence that speaks to more meaningful beauty; meaning that means something to you.

BELIEVING IN YOUR BEAUTIFUL BODY

You don't have to go far to find people pointing out statistics and personal experiences that show looks are the main thing that matter. It's brutal to think this way. It lacks creativity. When you know in your own heart you don't believe it, can't believe it, don't live that way, and don't deal with others like this, it's torturous to absorb this thinking as anything, but poisonous. As long as you have any kind of freedom to make your own choices, you don't have to succumb to what statistical data tells you. You choose what to accept and not accept in your life.

You can use information that is about the masses as the indication you can make a different plan for your own life. For example, setting up your life in a way you own using your personal power through side hustles or more intense entrepreneurial endeavors to build value around you on your terms, is a way to begin to write your own life terms differently. It's one of the very choices I made for some of these very reasons.

Externalizing your value and subscribing to the idea your worth is determined by the power of your facade, sends you walking a path toward misery. How can a person not crumble under that kind of weight at some point? If this idea was true, virtually everyone at some point in their lives would not be worth getting to know. That sounds ridiculous. It is a rare human who looks incredible all the time. That said, even if they do, that doesn't mean you want to expose yourself to them much as ugly can be an attitude.

Some people get the benefit of having assumed competence. You look at them and given their appearance which is put together and fitting an unoriginal, but easily identifiable quick to categorize mold, many around them assume they're competent human beings. It seems to create a kind of cultural entitlement in them even if they're decent people at heart. Many people can't possibly fully grasp challenges they avoid with the 'pass' they get with their assumed competence.

> ## Many people can't possibly fully grasp challenges they avoid with the 'pass' they get with their assumed competence.

I found myself in this position in my television career. I looked pretty enough without constructing a plasticized image. It gave me a pass. I was able to just be me professionally, because I had no overtone of 'How did you get that job?' or 'What makes you think you're so special?' I looked like I could be on television. I had assumed competence. I was there, because to know me is to understand I'm a professional communicator which manifests as a curious writer, creative storyteller, and emotionally engaged interviewer with a justice-minded nature. Journalism and independent producing have been a logical fit career-wise. With assumed competence came opportunity. The opportunity wasn't to benefit me. It was to my advantage when it could work that way, but my celebrity in that time as a television journalist with daily news output that resulted in my leading multiple newscasts on a daily basis upped my stock in ways others felt they could benefit and, as a result, I had invitations coming in left and right. I was afforded assumed competence. My empathy and realism are significant, so I could appreciate it and, yet, see it for what it was which is why I have the perspective I do today.

Many people work very hard to have nobody give them kudos. I had already made the connection myself and knew I had the benefit of the doubt in many ways given my position and how I held that position. Fortunately, I wasn't a person to abuse it. I could see, though, how easily positions of power get abused and kept my thinking in touch with struggles of others. I stand up for the underdog. It's my DNA. No matter how compassionate you are, however, it's virtually impossible not to lose track of at least some of that benefit, because habits breed expectations and expectations in how we're received involve a routine we learn to rely on. It lends itself to losing sight of yourself if you let it.

Having to navigate more difficulty gives you the opportunity to become a deeper, more discerning person. You're afforded chances to think differently, to hone skills differently. You have more opportunities or challenges, depending on how you view it, to find clever solutions to work around those with that benefit of the assumed competence. In time, if you value trend-of-the-day looks shoved at you as black and white social definitions of beauty, it can set up life as a merely transactional operation if a person isn't careful. We're better than that and more than that as a people.

Your beauty is yours, your body is yours, and it's a privilege when you offer any part of yourself to others.

Your beauty is yours, your body is yours, and it's a privilege when you offer any part of yourself to others. If it's not received that way, you haven't found your people yet. Keep moving forward.

LESSONS FOR THE ROAD:
1-Don't compare yourself to other women.
2-Don't judge other women based on appearance.
3-Don't participate in cruel chats that evaluate female body shape, including your own chats with yourself.
4-Limit contaminating mass media consumption.
5-Remember what others say tells you who they are, not who you are.

Rethink Challenge: Recognize when you reduce beauty to a narrow idea, it's a type of discrimination. Sometimes, that discrimination is against yourself. When someone is judged for their appearance on standards that aren't even possible given genetics above all, you have to decide if that is useful to the life you want to live moving forward. One more redefinition challenge is to see beauty in your texture as a human being. You are a patchwork of experiences, scars, joys, fits and starts in your life. Look for ways to embrace that. Stand strong in your own shoes no matter their size. Look for ways to live life as the best expression of YOU you can build, without allowing outside voices to decide for you. You have beauty, because you are here.

BETRAYAL

Self-betrayals are the only avoidable kind.

WHEN YOU GO UNDER

Have you ever hurt so badly, you weren't sure you could ever see your way out, because it came from a direction you least expected it? Have you ever been leveled and each time you tried to stand up you were knocked down again? Have you ever been in so much psychological pain, it became physical pain?

This chapter is the most challenging one for me to write. When you look at the snapshot of my life in the pages of this book as a whole, some reasons this topic became so painful for me likely become clearer.

I was brought up in a midwestern Irish Catholic home, the fifth of six kids and divorce was not in my vocabulary. Well, it was in the 'other' sense, as in other people experienced it. It was against God's plan for us. Like it or not, that's what I learned. It might seem plenty simplistic, but the clarity was useful at the time. I didn't sidetrack myself with other notions and relationship set-ups as a kid. There was never much to discuss. The assumed logic against divorce looked like this: I have a responsibility to keep my word, children need the stability of marriage, and divorce tears families apart.

We never discussed how to navigate ends of marriages or even what leads to ends of marriages. I don't think most people I knew growing up, whether religious, spiritual, or neither had much, if any, dialogue, on the matter even when facing those difficulties head on holding their various dysfunctions as the vast majority of us do. At very most, it was a unit of study in a one semester class that might not even be mandatory. Personally, I had no script for the walk. None. I entered into marriage with the commitment of the planets to its sun. My role was to assume my place as sometimes one of those planets, sometimes all of them, and sometimes as the sun depending on what the relationship required. My task was to be flexible, conscientious, loving, fun, adventurous, and willing to learn. It was about having a team spirit. It looked a little like this…

.....I will enthusiastically enter marriage with a whole heart ready for anything and as part of a thoughtfully chosen capable team where we each know this beautiful union is taking us to the grave together in our old age with grandchildren, lovely stories, countless adventures, playful spirits, and pure, deep, honest, growth-focused love that's mutually respectful and full of new discovery together....

Go ahead and laugh. It's syrupy. It's a good illustration of my sincerity entering marriage. There's a faction of the world, as in some idealists, who view this approach to life as possible and are doing it. Those who jeer that faction of idealists might not realize idealism is, in fact, instrumental in moving a culture forward. You have to be a visionary to see possibility and believe its doable to find a way to reach it yourself and help point others to it.

You have to be a visionary to see possibility and believe its doable to find a way to reach it yourself and help point others to it.

The institution of marriage might not always look the way it used to as we progress in this time. A heart-honoring approach to any relationship is valuable, nonetheless, should you choose to have one. My view was keep your word or don't commit. It was pretty much that simple and common sense to me. It sounds punitive, but it didn't apply to every aspect of marriage, just the trust aspect of it which is a huge piece of the pie.

Given this marriage long belief, it might be surprising there came a day I actually decided to leave my 20-plus year marriage. I was walking into the abyss scared as can be I'd never survive it, but knowing it was my only true chance for my soul's survival to live the way I wanted my life to pan out. I had learned plenty over the years including respect for the strength and power of my own voice as a woman.

NOBODY STRIVES FOR AN UNFULFILLING LIFE

This is an awful topic. Betrayal is disorienting, embarrassing, humiliating, and traumatic. I don't care how much self-esteem a person has, when you care you hurt walking through betrayal. Unless you go through it personally I'm not sure it's possible to imagine the pain. I'm not sure I could have fully appreciated it. Understanding something intellectually is a far cry from experiencing it emotionally.

Understanding something intellectually is a far cry from experiencing it emotionally.

I've been torn about whether to include this chapter in this book. It's raw. It's painful. It's human condition stuff and it's way bigger than me. I don't know that I have much to offer on the topic. I certainly have waded through it's mucky muddy waters which for good stretches of time felt more like drowning in sludge without as much as an ounce of grace to show for it at times. I do think I've done a decent job of navigating it in enough ways that I can, at least, offer some comfort and, if lucky, an iota of useful insight. Plus, it's no small accomplishment in growth to be able to stand in my own experience without feeling my duty is to everyone except me as if my choice to share ought to instead be an apology that I wasn't all-knowing enough to keep it from happening or, worse yet, keep from feeling so deeply hurt by it to maintain status quo and, thus, shamefully, hide the humanness of it all. I am just me and this is now part of my story.

Despite plenty of softening and healing that's taken hold, our family still lives the ripple effects of betrayal in having decided to divorce with two young kids and having that divorce mean a significant career shift for me that took time, resilience, and reinvention. Plus, I still feel the residue of stinging words from scorched earth arguments that continue to ring in my ears. I feel lingering remnants of shredding rejection in my heart that resulted from it all. The accusations. The disappointments. The confusion. The tangled and tattered trust. It's ugly stuff. It's not tidy and it's sad - so very sad. But then reality is sometimes sad. Time helps, but gratitude for the good around you seems to be a primary antidote.

Time helps, but gratitude for the good around you seems to be a primary antidote.

We often work hard to create thoughtful deliberate structures of love and safety around us. Sometimes we realize we're not where we thought we were and it's devastating to have to experience the blows and shifts necessary to take life in new directions. For those working their way through this kind of aching, I hope my perspective can offer some solace, despite the fact these scenarios are so individually tender.

To those who have not experienced a significant betrayal, I'm glad for you because it is one of the most excruciating experiences, if not the most difficult, to bounce back from for many people.

Betrayal is an intensely personal agony. It's one of the worst kinds of distress a human can endure. Making sense of it, whatever it's type, can feel impossible. One of those reasons is because you can't put a puzzle together when you're missing some of the pieces. Pieces, it's possible, nobody has to give you.

SELF-BETRAYAL VS. SELF-BLAME
Redirecting focus from breaches that hurt us so deeply is possible with time and by stopping betrayals we control.

> Redirecting focus from breaches that hurt us so deeply is possible with time and by stopping betrayals we control.

Every time you don't agree with something happening around you, you're in the range of committing a tiny betrayal against yourself. Over time and after many of these moments, conditioning can desensitize us to this habit.

Betrayal is a big idea. In fact, it's one of the biggest when it comes to adversity we're challenged to overcome. It's because every single word this book takes on is encompassed in the idea of betrayal. It's that big.

The dream is that we might be able to control betrayal and make it fixable. I've learned it's possible if we view our responsibility to ourselves as eliminating self-betrayal. If we shift our personal focus to betrayals we commit against ourselves instead of those done to us, we take on this topic in a constructive, useful way for our own personal thriving. Some people would find this idea offensive perceiving this offer as self-blame. But, blame is reactionary and comes at us from an un-empowered place. Staying in touch with those things that lead us into self-betrayal is proactive and empowering for forward movement through adversity. We see and own we are in enough control of our own destiny that we can impact change we seek around us. But, you have to let go of a few things. No thing is more important than what you need for your sense of self to remain intact. You can't externalize your value to achieve the goal or you betray yourself to please others. You have to know your values and commit to honoring those values in how you live life.

You have to know your values and commit to honoring those values in how you live life.

Self-betrayal is about all of the little things that lead us to decisions that cross our personal boundaries in tiny, seemingly insignificant ways. With each boundary crossing, we're in danger of betraying what we require for us by telling ourselves, "It's ok. It wasn't that important to me. I can adjust. I can just do it myself later. That person probably didn't mean to forget what they said they'd do. I don't think they'd hurt me intentionally. I'm not the center of the universe. Who am I to think my needs supersede everything and everyone else?"

You're not superseding everything and everyone else if what you request is reasonable, you're kind, ask for what you want, and the other person agrees then claims to forgot or chooses not to inform you before they flake. This is an example of red flag behavior.

Self-betrayal here is to say to yourself when you don't get a constructive response, "oh well, it wasn't that big a deal. This person just doesn't remember things very well. It's ok. I don't have guts to say directly this doesn't work for me, so I'll stew and not deal with it." You betray yourself if you aren't careful. The appropriate response from them is kindness and gentleness toward you when they realize they let you down. Is that what you're receiving? If not, why do you allow it?

The only option you seem to have is to control your own behavior, observe words, and actions of others, and then plan your life accordingly. If it sounds like a nutty idea to hold someone accountable for every little thing asked when they don't hold up their end of the bargain, it won't feel that way for long. The goal is for it to become second nature with you fully acting on the idea you're always worthy of kind consideration. It doesn't have to be more complicated than that. This has been one of the most important lessons of my adult life. You can understand this intellectually, but have difficulty fully integrating it into your requirements for yourself when it comes to your emotional experience. That's how it worked for me.

You pay attention, communicate your needs, correct misunderstandings, and let the other person show you who they are. If you learn you aren't a priority and requests continue to go unanswered, then accepting the behavior puts you in a position of betraying yourself.

CONFUSING SELF-BETRAYAL & SELF-BLAME

Self-blame after betrayal is different. It involves taking a moment when someone flakes on you such as the prior scenario saying, "Oh, it's me. I didn't ask for what I wanted clearly enough. Maybe I didn't communicate well enough. I didn't stay on it and keep checking. I asked too much." Plus, if your pattern is troubled enough with the other person, you hear their words telling you you're too sensitive and need to get over it or deal with it yourself which adds to the mental mess of it all. It feels like yuck just writing that. Self-blame sets you up for self-esteem destruction. It can't do anything else.

> Self-blame sets you up for self-esteem destruction. It can't do anything else.

We want to help people, give them the benefit of the doubt, care, love, give, share, try, try harder, find ways, communicate, learn and grow. It's awesome if the people in the relationship are equally invested in this way. But, if you aren't, and time is often the revealer, you decide if you'll stand up for you or set that aside in favor of navigating the other person. Whatever you accept, continues.

There's an idea betrayal is merely between the two people in the relationship and no one else. To absorb and believe that idea in and of itself would have been a self-betrayal for me personally when I heard it. Human beings impact each other and I know of not one case of different kinds of betrayal that did not impact children, family, and friends surrounding the couple no matter the range of the overstepping from intimate to financial choices. People are not islands. To accept the idea what's happening around us isn't happening is a prime example of self-betrayal.

I'd have been denying a reality I was living in my new landscape with all of the different people in my life. This idea that betrayal is only between the couple in the relationship felt like white board theory, not real life that involves emotions and the day to day of real live human beings. It came across like smoke and mirrors thinking as in, "You know all of the domino effects you're experiencing? That's not actually happening." Why would I want to gaslight myself was my thinking. Yes, you're experiencing fallout and others who love you are also experiencing their own version of adjustment afterward, particularly children even without spoken words. It was counter-intuitive to view it any other way in my experience.

We live in a culture that wisely requires children be treated well in all situations as we learn more about growth and development. If they aren't, very often someone is held accountable. When it comes to betrayal, there seems to be a lot of blank stares and shrugging about whether you can even claim children are impacted by betrayal in some circles because it's supposed to only be between the parents. If a family is driving down the road and the parents are disagreeing as the one driving suddenly angrily accelerates to 100 mph, the kids in the back seat are impacted and are in danger. The scene in the front seat still impacts them even though they were not directly involved. They are certainly along for the ride.

Human beings feel safe in answers, especially simple ones.

Human beings feel safe in answers, especially simple ones. If there were simple answers to betrayal, it would've been boxed up and sold for millions by now.

What's important to know is this. You cannot force another

55

person to betray you. Your personal power is about paying attention to moments you have the choice whether or not to betray yourself. If a scene won't change, you can choose to remove yourself from it. All of us operate at different frequency levels shifting as we grow and age. It goes high and low, up and down, in and out. People do what they feel and think they can. You decide what does and doesn't work for you.

A SLICE OF MY LIFE

In my own relationship, once our first child came more than 11 years into the marriage, I sought counseling to figure out why I cried so much feeling unhealthy, frustrated, confused, so so tired, and incredibly sad. There were likely baby blues in play. But, this was a significant life shift all the way around. I also now know those earliest stages of feeling unseen and dismissed were ultimatum time.

We'd be so much better off if our learning about relationships was summed up in a serious required mandatory series of classes as teenagers. So many of us spend so much more time in all kinds of relationships than in our specific jobs. I'd even go so far as to say it'd benefit the economy.

People who understand their value and know how to be self-sufficient and independent from the first years of their adulthood without relying on anyone else to keep a roof over their heads are well-positioned to help keep the economy stable. They know they can always find a way to make it on their own seeing less value in staying out of fear. It can't possibly hurt a person to know how to stand up for themselves.

My optimism and energy were waning in my relationship dynamic and it wasn't okay. I was in a situation where as years passed, it felt as though anyone except me was receiving growing bits of time, care, and attention I yearned for, particularly when pregnant with child number two and, ultimately, caring for two children as a career professional. I had to save myself. I was the only one who could do it. That marriage template I was handed as a child didn't include giving ultimatums or walking out, so it took a long time to make peace with these ideas. Being solution-focused, I had no idea solutions were impossible in the dynamic. I didn't have the tools to recognize that disconnect. I had to learn that with time.

As part of my own journey through betrayal, I learned there's a reason you don't have to go far to find the topic dangled in front of the masses like a horror or suspense movie. This is a type of dungeon most people can only think about experiencing in a dark anonymous movie theater which is not always the best training ground for empathy. Screens have a way of protecting us from having to feel life as deeply as can benefit us in our pursuit of intimacy.

Screens have a way of protecting us from having to feel life as deeply as can benefit us in our pursuit of intimacy.

People like to gossip about betrayal and broken promises of all kinds reducing the experiences to trite thoughtless certain sentences to entertain and distance themselves from the horrendous emotional impact of it all or to keep it black and white in their own minds. It makes sense, because it's full of unknowns which is scary. I have also wondered if focusing on your trouble takes attention off of their own relationship difficulties. After all, what people say tells you who they are, not who you are. It takes boundless courage to look closely at our own relationships.

I know it feels cruel and unfair when it becomes that kind

of chatter, but people are just people as a friend gently reminds me and something I tell my children in their own frustrations. That we are, myself included. I do believe in the deepest part of my being that, for the most part, people do the best they can do. Love in word, thought, and action is the only remedy no matter how far away we choose to distance from the object of our care. Or, some of us decide, at some point, to move on if the person and dynamic are toxic as can often be the case after these sorts of breaches of trust.

Whenever you mindfully choose something that significantly shifts the landscape around you, you'll be criticized and sometimes ostracized. That's a price we pay to progress as human beings.

> # Whenever you mindfully choose something that significantly shifts the landscape around you, you'll be criticized and sometimes ostracized. That's a price we pay to progress as human beings.

There can't possibly be signs for 100% of all relationship betrayal cases everywhere. There are too many factors at play for that to be possible. To think otherwise, makes us bigger and more arrogant than chance. I can't think that way. Sometimes problems are merely bigger than us and we can't do anything about it, despite best conscientious efforts. This can be difficult to internalize, but I invite you to dwell on this one idea. It made a huge difference in my own healing and maybe it can help you, too.

There's no dishonor in having guts to feel and care about other people, even if they might distance themselves from having to join you at that level of vulnerability. When visions for your mutual future don't align, keep moving forward. Trust the process.

TRUTH ONLY HURTS ONCE

Personal experiences are different for everyone. Some people hold broken trust as a dealbreaker and others don't. Some feel more strongly about one kind or another, while others think they're all unacceptable. To get into the nitty gritty of what I experienced is something I've grappled with in writing this book.

My difficulty in how betrayal is handled in the national conversation is that the discussion gets too easily sidetracked into inconsequential weeds of the topic. In talking about this subject, I have to keep in mind potential self-betrayals of my own sharing. My first consideration has always been how I can help and how my words can be useful in a broader conversation without impacting my children in a negative way. They're still kids. However, information is not usually the enemy. What we do with it can be in what I've witnessed through the years.

Giving clout to insensitivity of those involved serves no purpose in my estimation, because most families deserve more respect than equalized playing fields with people so disrespectful and disrespected they're kept a secret. People in affairs have their own growth journeys, but it's not the same path my children are walking in their young formative years. Because of this, keeping this topic to a more general awareness is enough as there are near universal impacts of betrayals that stand, no matter individual differences. Make no mistake, it can trigger a deep pain so profound, it can morph into physical pain that knocks you off your feet.

I will always want to know the truth of what is happening around me, but that doesn't mean that truth will always be ideal. I want to live a life that's real and seeing what's real around me is a big part of it. There's a saying about the idea that truth hurts once, but lies hurt every time you think about them and that seems like much the case from my vantage point. Plenty of people prefer to handle these topics in different ways than I did and I get it. Everyone has different situations and different desires and requirements. I'm a free spirit with a strong moral compass and, fortunately or unfortunately, divorce is giving my story a more authentic ending. I never would've imagined that plot twist when mixing my DNA with learned devotion to my commitments. It's important to make distinctions between the innate goodness in a human being and behavior they choose despite facing the fact you have to set limits for your own equilibrium sometimes. It comes down to value systems.

It could be suggested that my having been raped in college or my deeply feeling personality, professional independence, ability too embrace logic in tandem with feeling, or the many harassments and violations of trust I've experienced over the years are why betrayal is such a painful topic for me or even the reason my marriage ended.

Maybe it happened because I'm able to make myself so vulnerable to someone I love that I create conditions for breaches with my ability to trust. After all, trusting none too rarely equals deep hurt eventually by some kind of leveling. It's no secret people are imperfect. So many possible causes rushed me like some kind of force of nature after I found out about the holes springing in my relationship and it didn't seem to stop for quite a while. We were sinking fast. It could be that I'm naive, gullible even, or it could be that I'm capable of seeing and striving for more making me that force of nature and that was the problem.

Or, it could just be that I can't control the decisions and perspectives of other people.

Vision is a hard place to live for many who can't risk

disappointment. I can and I do because I feel and I think with hope. I must feel to know I'm living a life worth living. Introspection is a necessity for my survival. An independent mind is my loyalty to myself.

An independent mind is my loyalty to myself.

I've learned that when you know where you end and where others begin, it can make you a tough case and a target for gossip and ridicule. Boundaries are not always welcome. I've reluctantly learned to accept the idea that some people are offended when you don't rely on a group to be you when they need the cover to make sense of their own choices. When that happens to me, I see it gently most of the time. I understand insecurity and fear and have walked through my fair share. If attempting to reduce and shame me is a route to more self-esteem for someone else I learned long ago, so be it. I control no one, but myself. I focus on keeping my words, thoughts, and actions aligned. It's my personal beacon of light no matter the ambiguity around me.

TRUST TENDER TRUTHS

As I tell my own kids, do your best to stay honest with yourself and truthful with others. You'll be lonely at times determined to do that and it's not always perfect, but building relationships on pretend versions of ourselves to gain favor means you're not actually known to people in your life. If you can build the inner strength to trust that you're enough alone, even when it's hard, while staying sincere in your dealings, and doing it with a discerning eye, you make space for the right kinds of people. You'll recognize each other and be glad to have held space for authentic connections. There are some people who when they don't like you it's to your credit. I truly believe that.

Peaceful co-existence is my go-to as a human being. However, I respect myself and love myself enough to not allow myself to be disregarded in my own life - at least not more than once or twice before I make changes. Sometimes that means cutting people off and when those times do happen, I'm not happy about it but do it with clarity and certainty. We must sometimes to maintain our own inner balance.

Intimate betrayal is the worst kind of vulnerability smash for my personality. It felt like all of the discussions, talks, agreements, desires, and beliefs didn't matter in the end. That said, I work hard to understand and see someone else's experience and my nature is to champion opportunities to live in harmony.

So what is a person like me to do? First, I'd like to make a hopeful guess that there are plenty of us. Second, as I said at the beginning of this section, I have no answers only personal awarenesses and experiences lived as a tangled delicate and dramatic dance between my heart and head.

Here's the trouble in a bigger sense in my estimation. As long as anything about humans is viewed as a commodity, we'll be at risk for discard, devaluing, and being used up - every last one of us.

Does it mean I can't be happy again or that I'm not happier now as I make new choices taking life in a new direction after betrayal and divorce? Not at all. I always knew I was capable of growth and reinvention.

What being devastated by betrayal feels like is that you weren't worth the truth to someone who was supposed to have your back. Actually, it's possible your partner didn't feel they were worth the effort to be truthful with themselves and you were merely in that path. Each relationship is it's own world. I remember a counselor saying partners in relationships usually have very different experiences in the dynamic over the years which was a mind-blowing idea to me. I had no idea that what seemed like reality from my vantage point could be perceived as sometimes the opposite by my spouse despite most sincere efforts otherwise on the part of each of us. One of the most precious experiences on the planet to me is being able to trust another person not thinking in terms of a win in the dynamic. When that trust is shattered, it feels terrible. Is trust a mirage then? Maybe it is, but I didn't and don't want to believe that and couldn't figure out how you put a crystal vase back together once it's been knocked to a stone floor.

I heard ideas from people outside of the relationship that I was too independent, too proud, being difficult, uppity, must think I'm special, and that my stock wasn't going to go up with time versus how it worked for men if I left the marriage. I was witnessing people speaking from where their own fears live, not the fears of others and, particularly, mine. We each have our own fears and insecurities to face over the years. I was aware I was living in a culture eager to give me, as a woman particularly, an expiration date after having been flagged as part of one of those seemingly, stable long time couples struggling at midlife and now setting off alarms because it looked like we were going down. Men are not the only ones who do it. Women are often primary culprits. I knew I had plenty of value as a woman and human being no matter what personal decisions I made for myself. The challenge was not letting the poison in from the outside. Human beings are not commodities to me. Forgiveness and unconditional love don't necessarily mean staying married. I knew, with time, those pieces could fall in place if it felt right whether or not I was still married. If I didn't believe in myself, who would believe in me?

Forgiveness and unconditional love don't necessarily mean staying married.

I have to give while living in hope, love, kindness, gentleness, and with trust that any partner I choose to include in my life feels the same way. For me, relationship glue is in the soft places, not the contractual ones we file in courthouses for the benefit and approval of the public.

I decided if I was alone for the rest of my life after divorce, but feeling peaceful and content in my surroundings, it'd be fine. I like who I am and in that knowing, I was aware that, in time, I'd be okay and I am. I had nothing to prove to anyone.

ONE DAY AT A TIME AS LONG AS IT TAKES

My best advice can be summed up this way: one moment at a time, one decision at a time, one day at a time for as long as it takes to fully stand up again. Sometimes, it feels like a very long time. It's personal and individual. For a long time, I went very internal to heal and focused on keeping life as simple as possible for my kids, eventually wanting at least one or two friends and family members to hold my hand at times through it until I felt strong again. Some people work very differently. It's such a personal seeking through healing.

Some cruelties have a shattering, life-altering effect on some of the kindest, most genuine, decent people among us capable of trusting people at their word. I don't want fewer of these people in the world as I often hear eluded to when it's said victims ought to have known better whatever their circumstances. We have endured and even championed a lot of entitled thinking culturally labeling it success. Calling it out to ourselves first is a vital primary line of defense. That requires we catch tiny self-betrayals that lead to more significant boundary crossing when someone is willing to dramatically, knowingly cause us pain. Going along to get along can be a dangerous philosophy.

Going along to get along can be a dangerous philosophy.

When it comes to betrayal, all of it starts with a lie. People usually lie to themselves before lying to anyone else thinking it's ok to be duplicitous, lie by omission, dismiss and deflect, knowingly saying something blatantly untrue. We are all challenged as human beings to keep our words, thoughts, and actions aligned as often as possible for our own peace of mind which is a legitimate selfish reason, if nothing else. The other misnomer is everyone is doing it. On the contrary, many of us are committed to staying truthful in our dealings.

While I don't have an exact answer that solves the frustrating and disheartening emotional conundrums as you move through betrayal, I offer this. You're not alone. Many people have endured relationship betrayal albeit at different intensity levels and over different periods of time, but confusion, anger, loss, hurt, sadness, and frustration are widespread results.

It's not about perfection. People lie. It's human. It's about personal values; knowing them and staying aligned to them. Missteps and mistakes happen, but course corrections are key. These are gateway decisions to extreme betrayals. If someone who has agreed to hold and protect your vulnerability attacks your value system with their choices, that's betrayal. It's pretty much terrifically awful to endure. I wish betrayal on no one.

Betrayal is one of the dreadful words and maybe one of the last as we get so used to the idea fewer and fewer words are taboo anymore. People use it to move plots along in movies basing entire shows around it. Counselors, attorneys, and detectives build entire lives around careers focused on it, in whatever form, because it's not fixable. Once performed, it can't be undone, whatever it's flavor. It's final. You either betray or you don't in a given situation. You either crossed a pre-determined red line or you didn't. It's a polarizing, fear-inducing, anger provoking word. There are few words like that that can pull such strong reactions out of people.

BETRAYAL'S BEAUTIFUL BONUS

Only a few months into my own disorienting profound relationship difficulties, I was in Charleston, South Carolina at a long time street market with my sisters and my mom shopping on one of our annual adventure trips together. A woman in one of the booths watched me closely as I perused her selection of books. It didn't take her but a few minutes to clue in to me with kindness. She gave me a book of inspired ideas to take with me as a companion on my trip home. It was her simple way of caring for another human being. Her kind eyes and gentle smile offered me social support that day. A stranger spotted my sad spirit and took care of my heart that day.

The only label I wore to her booth was the one we all wear. The invisible writing on it said fellow human being. Her compassion made such a difference for me in that moment. I still remember it and continue to cherish our quiet exchange years later. She knew I was living in a new direction by what I was dwelling on and wanted to support me on my journey having been there herself. You have that secret ability now. You have a new insight that involves healing powers which can benefit those hurting around you and it's an awesome gift.

Whether or not you find betrayal had a silver lining for you turning into a useful catalyst, depends on what you value in life. Whatever the case, you have the opportunity to drive a new vision for the world once you've been betrayed because you are forced to look at life from a new vantage point. Your healing can heal others because of your empathy and compassion for yourself. Here's why. Being, basically, forced to tap your own self-love as a survival mechanism after such extreme pain gives you a road map to help others find the way also.

> Being, basically, forced to tap your own self-love as a survival mechanism after such extreme pain gives you a road map to help others find the way also.

You've been granted a precious vision for the potential of a better future and you know how to walk with others on that arduous excruciating journey. I recognize those around me hurting from this kind of pain more easily now.

Congratulations. What you thought would lead to your certain demise has given you a vantage point from which to lead others through their own pain. You can be a new kind of beacon of hope and light for those you encounter now. Helping those struggling more than we are is the only certain good in life in my estimation.

Rethink Challenge: We cannot make collective sense of betrayal as a culture. It holds dichotomies. Is a person who betrays all bad? Most likely not. Is a person who betrays someone we want to continue to be around? It depends. Then there's self-betrayal. We let our own lives slip out from under us when we allow ourselves to work against what we want. Some never get out from under the weight and residue of betrayal. Some move on with ease. Some lie to themselves and others not to have to face it. It's tough disrupting stuff - some of the toughest. You had nothing to do with another

person choosing to hurt you this way. As grown ups, we are responsible for our decisions. To think you have any control over another's decisions is, in and of itself, controlling behavior which makes that line of thinking nonsensical from my perspective. Your decisions now are to decide what you want for your life and identify ways you betray yourself learning to stop working against yourself. Plus, be one of the helpers to others you recognize along the path knowing well what they have before them.

FORGIVENESS

*Forget forgiveness to give
your mind space for it.*

FORGIVING THE UNIVERSE

When my daughter was 11 months old, I noticed what I thought were rug burns on the tops of her feet from crawling around on carpet. I took her to the doctor opening the door to a world we knew nothing about and became one of the most frustrating journeys of our lives.

Lucy was diagnosed with eczema. It's considered a nuisance condition, but there are complications that can and have happened to her. In fact, she overcame a tough case of MRSA it was believed entered her body through broken skin related to eczema landing her in the emergency room when a doctor was concerned the infection was moving toward her heart. Eczema not only impacts quality of life for her and others in the house, it can also impact a child's self-esteem. It's not curable, so the solution seems ambiguous. Sourcing can be tough as hers is, so it's managed, not fixed. Little to no sleep is the standard situation many nights when you have a child with a severe eczema flare up. You find yourself looking at bloody sheets often and there are lots of tears. It's difficult to comfort a child who can't relax, because of the constant itching with no cure in sight. You soothe her with hugs, lotions, ointments, ice packs, medicine, distractions, wraps, oil baths, stroller walks, you name it. It's relentless and peace is an ethereal idea that seems to mock you from a distance.

People would ask what was wrong with her in public. They could say surprisingly insensitive things to this beautiful, gleeful child. I'm referring to adults, not children. We'd hear questions such as, "What's wrong with her face?" "What happened to her?" She didn't think she was any different until she heard those kinds of responses to her presence.

When she was three years old, she started singing constantly and sang her way through everything. It's an awesome aspect of how she works and she has always had a beautiful voice. In fact, while shopping in a department store one day a woman stopped me saying she was a music teacher, Lucy had a great voice, and must keep singing. That woman made my day having no awareness we were in a flare up at that time. Her kind words were a beacon of light of their own and a welcome change in subject for my tired mind. Eczema issues are hard to escape, because they never seem to go away always on alert for the next flare up. I believe Lucy's singing was a function of her creative coping and, during that time, it kicked in to save her spirit, as creativity often does for many of us.

Lucy's pre-school teacher thought she had an attention disorder at one point. It's something we heard from multiple teachers over the years. She was fidgety with a short attention span during eczema flare ups. I told the teacher what I believed was happening. She hadn't heard of eczema being that severe. Lucy's attention troubles coincided with flareups on a regular basis. This is just one more indication of the ripple effect this so-called nuisance condition can spark. It became a central focus. How can you create a safe space for your child, when they don't even feel safe in their own skin? How good does a child feel in a class where they get behind because of their physical discomfort, something most of us have the good fortune of being able to take for granted most of our lives? How can it not affect a child to have kids want to play with you today, but shun you a week later if your skin looks distracting and you sit around itching your body to cope while at school? A child learns to self-protect. How could you not?

HOLIDAY IN THE HOSPITAL

During the Spring, before Lucy went into Kindergarten, she got her school physical. She was excited to start school as a bright curious little girl with a stunning internal fantasy world. In fact, one of the first things she said about her teacher the first day was that she smelled like stars and Lucy decided she wanted to be a rainbow when she grows up. Lucy has always had a little magic in her spirit. It's the kind of thing, as a parent, you want to protect, because you know it's her idealism mixed with playfulness that gives her such a beautiful outlook. I've filled pages with quotes of her perspective on life in that time and it's an awesome memento. I still benefit from her fantasy world thinking even today. Again, I believe creativity can save us sometimes.

It wasn't but a couple weeks after her school physical that we were in the doctor's office again, when she had unexplainable stomach pains. In the middle of eating her meal, she dropped to the kitchen floor clutching her stomach and wailed. It was alarming. I took her to the doctor that same day in mid-June. Her doctor at the time thought her stomach pain equaled constipation and sent the two of us home. I wasn't satisfied. Something wasn't right and it was not constipation. I knew what constipation was in a child and this was not that. We followed protocol, but I wasn't done figuring it out. Lucy had stomach pain a couple of times in following days and while it hurt her, she didn't double over the way she did the first time. It was a mystery.

Two weeks later on a camping trip with friends in northern Illinois, Lucy couldn't sleep in the night and was in excruciating pain. She came out of her room asking for help. Our concern was starting to fly off the charts. That morning, we headed to the closest doctor and because we were now in the 4th of July holiday weekend, we wound up in a nearby hospital emergency room. I was determined not to walk out pacified with the directive to fix what was earlier assumed to be constipation.

We were no sooner in an individual room with Lucy on a gurney, when the on-duty doctor walked in, scanned her body in her spaghetti strapped fuchsia tank and jean shorts immediately alluding to the idea she was being physically abused. Her skin was having a flare up. Looking at her red rashing skin, scabbing on her legs, and watching her periodically doubling over in abdominal pain, he said in front of her in the observation room with the nurse by his side, "What is happening to this child?" throwing his arms up in exasperation.

It wasn't the first time it'd had been wrongly assumed we were mistreating her. It hurt every time, but I understood the concern and appreciated the desire to protect a child. I explained the situation telling the doctor she has severe eczema which we were told was one of the worst cases her doctor's office had seen and was separate from the reason we were there. I said we're open to whatever advice you can provide on her eczema, because we can't make it go away having had at least six different doctors look at it in different clinics and hospitals in different cities between primary, dermatologists, and allergists trying to solve it, but it wouldn't go away.

During the conversation, the doctor had an out of the blue hunch he told us later and decided to do another test. He discovered her intestine was collapsing in on itself. She had an intussusception. She wasn't the standard demographic for the condition and her primary doctor across the state told us later, she would have never caught it. We were incredibly fortunate that particular doctor in that emergency room in the particular community that particular day had his hunch. From there, the scene changed, the pace picked up, and movement was brisk. They knew what they were looking at and that meant they could waste no time.

They said she had to be Life Flighted to the nearest trauma center right away before gangrene set in to her intestines which left her with a poor prognosis if they didn't remedy this right away. I watched them wheel out my little girl with her long curls and impish grin, strapping her to the gurney with several belts. It actually looked like what I imagine a military operation might look like in trying to get someone out of harm's way in a helicopter. We said goodbye, as she took in everything around her with confusion and curiosity. We stood on the cement outside of the hospital as the helicopter lifted off the very big cement slab with our very little girl inside.

We followed the helicopter to the hospital. We were on the interstate and it was high above us eventually out of our view as it moved on ahead. My heart was in my stomach and I was about as frightened as I've ever been feeling powerless with a sense this family was in free fall. It was scary for all of us. Liam was three-months-old and silent in his carseat eventually drifting off to sleep. Lucy's dad and I were quiet most of the ride with no way to know what to expect next. We never anticipated this result and were overwhelmed.

Lucy was already at the hospital when we arrived and within an hour or two, they blew out her intestine by putting a hose in her bottom with no pain killers. They heard her wailing. It was awful to watch and, no doubt, worse to experience. They said they didn't want pain killers masking what she felt. Her reactions helped them know what was happening inside her body. It seemed to do the trick. Her cries came and they assessed accordingly. We talked about it when she was in junior high. She remembers most of it, but not that part of the whole ordeal which I wasn't disappointed to hear.

They watched her intestine saying if it telescoped again, they'd have to operate. It did telescope again a few hours later. Her dad left shortly after we arrived to fetch our vehicle at the campsite where we left it hours away, so the start of the next week would be a bit less scattered with little clarity what we were in for everything was so moment to moment.

It was the middle of the night and I was alone with the baby getting news they had to do an emergency surgery thinking it was the wisest plan. However, it is the stars can align, that was the moment my older brother, Mick, walked in to the hospital room. As soon as he heard what was happening, he hit the road to be available and he was a sight for sore eyes. I was alone and couldn't take the baby with me to be near Lucy, but the baby couldn't be alone either. My brother arrived in exactly enough time for me to hand him the baby as I was escorted to the surgery prep area where Lucy was being wheeled. Mick held the baby for hours in the room dozing in and out waiting for word as we all were, about his niece.

As they prepped her, they asked me to pick out a special cap for her as standard protocol and sweet gesture as I was picking from elastic caps that look like a shower cap in various fabrics. They were made by caring volunteers and, in that, I felt great comfort. I felt so helpless and this gave me something, just anything I could do. I picked a bright rainbow-color one covered in flowers in hope I'd see that same kind of beautiful bright spark in my girl again after this procedure. She was exhausted by the whole ordeal and, at four years old, wanted it over and wanted her stomach to stop hurting. She was quiet during the entire surgery prep experience, two parts tired and 10 parts brave. I watched them wheel her away as a wave of helplessness washed over me. Waiting was all I could do. Patience.

Her surgery started after midnight and lasted until after 2a. They removed part of her large and small intestines, her appendix, and the flap between the intestines that controls food moving through the body.

When I woke up having accidentally dozed off in a deserted waiting room waiting for her dad to get back to the hospital and waiting for word on the outcome, I was disoriented and panicked. I've never had the feeling before or after quite like the feeling I had when I woke up disoriented in that empty waiting room in the middle of the night. I felt like I was losing myself, going under, getting pulled into the undertow of the moment, having a very unfamiliar panic attack as I didn't know where my child was, what had happened, and how I could have fallen asleep?! How could I sleep when my child was in surgery? Her dad was awake, too, and we hurried to a phone asking for guidance on what was happening. The nurse on the other end was able to put our minds at ease that Lucy was out of surgery and back in her room sleeping herself, as well. They saw no reason to wake us up.

When I saw her in her room, she looked like a beautiful sleeping doll with a head full of long big curls in her thin hospital gown. But, this doll had IVs and a catheter curled up peacefully on the bed sleeping with the glow of outside light peaking into the room through the window. She barely spent any time awake for two days. Her body was wiped out. So were we. That first night after surgery was 4th of July evening and her room overlooked a river that would feature the fireworks display. Lucy had a front row seat. After a full day of sleep with barely any consciousness from her, we wheeled her bed over next to the window and I talked to her about all of the pretty fireworks as she continued to rest. For just a few moments, she woke long enough to see the show outside as I helped her lift her head just a few inches off her pillow saying, "I see the pink ones, mommy. They are so pretty." And, she fell back asleep. That was enough. My heart swelled for her.

It wasn't but another couple of days and the spontaneous singing she did constantly and had for nearly two years came back again after having gone away the day we headed to the emergency room. I never heard a sweeter sound in my life than this sweet child finding her song again. Our girl was on her way back.

During Lucy's after care doctor appointments, she was given the sign off as a healthy little girl. While it would take some time for her body to fully heal, we went ahead and sent her to kindergarten, as planned. We had no sooner done that than, than Liam became unusually ill.

LITTLE ONES NEVER NEED FORGIVENESS

At a doctor appointment the first couple days of Lucy being in school, it was thought Liam had a mild virus, but through the night into the next day it became worse. He'd developed a full body rash and had become so lethargic he no longer looked at anyone. He lay there making a weak noise over and over paying no attention to presence in the room. I was scared and took him back to the doctor.

As soon as his primary doctor walked in, I could tell by his reaction we had a big problem. He immediately looked at me and said, "How long has he been like this?" When I was there with him the day before, this doctor hadn't been available, so one of the lead doctors in the clinic saw him instead. I said, "He seems worse today and that's why I'm here. Something isn't right." He said, "I'll be right back." He brought back the other doctor and they decided within a minute or two he had to get to the children's hospital the next city over. My doctor looked at me and said, "If you can't get him there in 45 minutes, we'll send him in an ambulance." I said, "We'll go right now."

My head was spinning and that feeling of my heart dropping into my stomach was back. I fastened the snaps of his little white onesie, lifted him off the exam table, and put him in his car seat fastening the seat belt as fast and tenderly as possible. He was still not interested in anything around him. His lethargy was so clear. I scurried with the car seat carrying my fading baby out of the office to the white Jeep Wrangler I was driving that day. I fastened him in the back, and hit the road knowing I had to get there in less than an hour. They were waiting for Liam in the emergency room.

The office called ahead to warn them we were coming. I called his dad and said, "You won't believe what is happening right now." And, he couldn't. I was still processing it myself. I was so scared and was headed back to the same hospital we had just left only weeks prior. Once I arrived, they whisked him out of my arms, took off all of his clothing and diaper, and laid him on a warm hospital baby examining table in the room we were assigned. Several people were gathered around him as I backed up not taking my eyes off of Liam and the doctors. I felt helpless again.

As that was happening, my older sister, Mary Zita, and my

mom walked in. They happened to be nearby when news came we were headed to the hospital and they rushed over. Doctors initially thought Liam had bacterial meningitis which added a dimension to the fear for everyone because that prognosis didn't look good. We were told he might not make it. He was given a spinal tap and the most intense medicine they can give a baby without killing him we were told by his medical team. In fact, I won't forget how they described the strong medications they put in my little boy with the words, "We are pulling out the big guns." It was a very long night. Any moment I could hold my baby, I held him. I sat with him for hours and hours thinking of all of the scenarios. I didn't want to miss a moment of his life. I didn't know how much more of it he had left to live.

Lucy and her dad came back and forth spending as much time as they could at the hospital between work and Lucy's first week in school. As time went on, his team began to doubt he had bacterial meningitis. It became increasingly confusing because he had so many different symptoms they told us and all of those together didn't fit just one diagnosable illness or disease. Here's what we knew. They counted 10 unexplained symptoms and he was a 5-month-old baby not improving. It was a head scratcher.

Because of his many seemingly-unrelated symptoms, we were quarantined in the room and visited by a Centers for Disease Control doctor to get to the bottom of his illness. They thought he might have H1N1. All told, several different ideas were batted around. He was in the hospital about a week. I stayed with him the whole time he was there in the same place his sister had been shortly before in the summer. The staff was stunned to see us back. He ended up having two viruses and two staph infections all at once - a fluke. Just like it was a fluke he fell so severely ill and he needed to be admitted to a hospital so soon after his older sister's hospital stay.

THE TIME IT TAKES

Lucy and Liam are happy healthy kids now and I love who they are as kind compassionate human beings. Lucy's eczema is still a tough case, at times, more often than I'd wish for her. It impacts her desire to get sweaty, to sit in grass, wear certain kinds of clothing, or do other things that so many of us take for granted. Something like sitting by a fire while camping can be annoying for her, because she's not looking for new reasons to dry out her skin with smoke to then find herself taking an extra shower also drying to her skin. Add to that, potential of mosquito bites and bug repellants no matter how mild and sunscreen during a summer outing and this child has had enough. It's been difficult at times not to have some un-focusable frustration and anger that she has had to endure so much already in her young life.

Some might say what's there to forgive? They are happy and healthy now! It's true, but sometimes you have to forgive the seeming unfairness when you are handed so much difficulty all at once. Only, with time do you see the light at the end of the treacherous tunnel. It's incredibly difficult to watch your child handle more than most adults and have to find her way through it.

> ### It's incredibly difficult to watch your child handle more than most adults and have to find her way through it.

I haven't talked about how that particular year impacted my marriage and family, but there was forgiveness needed there, too, as some people find it easy to be supportive in tough times and they are gems, while others don't have that willingness or ability. There can be emotional residue in a marriage after difficult circumstances and no matter how grateful and thankful you are, you can still be stung by the insensitivity around you. I understand people do what they can, nobody is perfect, and I could change things about myself, too. But, when you walk through painful times, tough stuff has a way of making realities crystal clear, particularly when it involves children who need the best we have to give as often as we can give it.

Many words and experiences make up this one idea of forgiveness. This word is used so patly to describe what can be an arduous journey of internal and external coping and seeking, clarity, and release over a long period of time.

I'm amazed by people who, shortly after a devastating blow, can jump to forgiveness with certainty. I never know how to absorb that idea, but it's their experience, their decision, and I admire that inner strength I have yet to discover in myself but observe with curiosity willing to learn.

I'm a forgiving person, but I want to understand and that's, most often, where my personal snags happen as sometimes that is an elusive idea. I'm astute and aware I have a right to hold space in the world. The difficult balance is in being able to forgive without turning into a doormat. I keep this in check. Maybe you relate, as well.

By the time you reach mid-life, there's a better than average chance you'll have found yourself face to face with the word forgiveness more than a few times. People and predicaments hurt you, sometimes badly. It's not hard to find reasons to be jaded and cynical, but the questions shift toward whether that serves you and your life quest. Anger is not a good permanent resident for your mind if you think ahead about the person you want to be in your own mental house of memories.

Anger is not a good permanent resident for your mind if you think ahead about the person you want to be in your own mental house of memories.

As a girlfriend long ago told me in relation to her own challenges in forgiving her father for disappointments in their relationship, she said, "You know what, Maria? To a decent extent, we control how others remember us." I never forgot it.

Here's some insight into my mind. I don't much like the word forgiveness. In fact, this is the word that kicked off my utter certainty a book like this could have value for many people.

Those 11 letters put together looking all tidy and easily tossed at people in times of excruciating pain as if you simply unpack the idea and... Voila - acceptance. It's too simple. I don't know about you, but I tend to feel worse hearing that right after a significant blow than if the person had said nothing. Hearing - you must forgive - can feel like a dishonoring of the crushing blows you've absorbed.

You can know a person's intentions are wonderful with advice to forgive, but the word can feel impossible to process when you're devastated. The heaviness of the word can be bigger than the resources you think you have to hold it.

It can feel like added weight to your shoulders which are already burdened navigating aftermath of whatever happened mixed with what you already balance in life. In my own life, I had to figure out a way to chuck forgiveness, so I could actually give it. It sounds counterintuitive.

> In my own life, I had to figure out a way to chuck forgiveness, so I could actually give it. It sounds counterintuitive.

Here's my personal process in hope it helps you, too. I toss aside the word forgiveness and untangle the emotions like this:

1- Reality - I accept the reality of what is. What you are living is reality, not what was hoped for or could have happened. This is your reality. This is now.

2- Release - I imagine myself actually releasing hurt into the sky like a bird flying away. My visualization might seem hokey to you, so choose what best fits you. Visualization helps make the process more tangible for me.

3- Respect - Having respect for our humanness and its utter imperfect execution at times is an art form. People hurt us because they're on their own journey, not ours. It's absolutely awful how much damage some people can do. There is no justice in it, so often, but I'm not convinced that's the point. Anyway, to go gentle on others in a healthy way, we have to have the balance of being able to go gentle on ourselves first. Some people might call this grace. There's beauty in the idea, however achieved. You are worthy of this kind of beauty in your life. It took me a while to see this step as a strength and not a weakness, but once I understood it's value and power, there was no looking back.

4- Relief - I have found by focusing on things other than forgiveness, specifically the steps above, forgiveness took care of itself. At some point, I realize it happened when I wasn't looking. What a relief to let it go.

One more thought: The idea there is grieving in forgiveness has helped me tremendously. This is something Author Brene Brown has talked about in her work. Knowing there is no specific time table for grieving relieves pressure giving me space to let forgiveness happen in it's own time, as well.

Rethink Challenge: Forgiveness isn't tidy. At least, it doesn't have to be. It doesn't have to be immediate to be valuable. It isn't about anyone else. It's about your willingness to accept a new reality that is different than you thought you were living at the time the adversity entered your life. Can you accept the reality of what is? That is the question my kind of forgiveness requires to be able to start to unravel this world and reweave it into a process I can actual get my head around. Forgiveness is a word that has too much caught up in it. We actually judge the value of others on how and if they forgive. Some like them better when they forgive and some like them less. Forgiveness isn't for other, though, and that's part of our learning. To forgive or not forgive, that is a personal question.

NORMAL

Everyone's normal is different.

THE NARRATIVE OF NORMAL

I was talking with a children's book expert recently discussing how we learn from books from early ages in ways that don't likely register with us. She talked about cultural narratives related to research I was doing for an upcoming digital media project I produce for a textbook author. One point she made was particularly powerful in relation to this chapter about the idea of normal. We are impacted by so many things in ways that don't immediately register which go into the collective pot that is our awareness of ourselves.

For example, my little sister and I are less than two years apart in age. There were periods in our childhood people treated us like twins. We are much different in personality and appearance, but did everything together and were often a matched set in the eyes of others. When we received gifts, there was a distinct pattern from my vantage point. She very likely has a different view herself. This is the beautiful and perplexing thing about normal. We each own our own.

Michelle received the more childlike, playful colors, patterns, and styles of whatever the item was, while I would get the more grown up looking colors, styles, or patterns because I was 20 months older. Think tan and maroon for me instead of bright pink and yellow she might receive. Sometimes, that bugged me. Even though I was four years old to her two years old, I still liked pink and yellow just as much in dolls as she did. I don't even think it was always a conscious choice by people in and outside of the family, because it happened so often. It might very well have contributed to my relatively serious nature. I can't know for sure, but I was getting some type of message as part of that cultural narrative. Normal isn't one path.

Normal isn't one path.

Besides that minor example, I didn't grow up in a family that could claim being normal in the larger cultural context at even the most shallow level. We were professional entertainers. My dad, Lee, was an art teacher with a master's degree at a time that wasn't common. My mom, Rita, was a lighthearted artistic woman who spent her life supporting our entertainment lifestyle with her creativity, resourcefulness, planning ability, and emotional support.

My parents tiptoed into professional entertainment well before they married. My dad mail-ordered a unicycle and taught himself to ride it in high school. He also taught himself magic and combined the two working his way through college with his creative and business skills. He began dating my mom when they were in high school together and when he went to college at the small private university nearby, she worked alongside him as his magician's assistant balancing another job eventually learning to ride the unicycle, as well.

He did all of this while spending nights taking turns with his father on shifts with their tractor working corn and soybean fields around their rural home. My dad worked the fields while my grandfather slept and took care of the younger boys. Then, dad spent days and evenings in classes, set up and worked shows, and helped his dad with his two little brothers catching sleep as he could.

Both of my parents lost their mothers when they were young. My mom had six kids and has always had a bright cheery nature weathering plenty along the way, not the least of which was losing her own mother during The Depression. Her mother, Mabel Marie, tripped and fell down the stairs in the night holding an oil lamp. This was in the late 1930's. My grandma was about 40 when she fell to the bottom of the stairs. The lamp ignited a carpet underneath her and she was terribly burned. My grandfather found her, rolled her body in a rug, and took her to the hospital that way.

My mother at eight-years-old and as one of eight children in her rural Illinois farm family was told at the hospital she could kneel and say a prayer next to her mother shortly before she passed away. She did and next thing she knew her mom was gone. From the age of eight, her life no longer fit the 'normal' mold. From there, she relied on her teenage sisters for motherly support.

My dad's mom, Zita Marie, died when he was a teenager months after going to Mayo Clinic to find a cure for the cancer they learned upon arriving had already ravaged her body. My dad told the story about his own father being instructed to bring his mom home to die. Doctors couldn't help her. Ultimately, she died weeks after an operation in a hospital near their rural home.

My dad was the oldest of three boys and took on responsibility at a young age due to the demands of the time, the needs of his family, and his own personality not to mention birth order. He was able to introduce my mom to his own mother one time on the night of a school dance. His mother, Zita, was also in her 40's and the loss of his mother when he was in high school devastated my dad. My mom had already gone through the significant loss of her own mother and the heartbreak that went with that years before. It's not difficult to see that that common experience added a dimension to their connection that helped glue their relationship together.

When times are difficult and answers are few, my mom's mantras learned from her parents are, 'There but for the grace of God go I' and The Serenity Prayer.

The peace it gives her helps us find peace at times no matter our religious or non-religious views as her children. There's quite a bit of beauty in the idea of grace.

Each of my parents found themselves having to get used to a new normal. It's possible shaking loose from former ways of existing opened them up more than ever to taking chances differently in how they decided to build an entertainment career around my dad's teaching lifestyle.

By the time I came along as the fifth child in the line of six, I was surrounded by human beings each sporting different creative skills and interests. We were unusual. I learned at about eight years old my family's lifestyle was different than any other kid I knew. I grew up on the road much of the year as the only life I knew until I left for college. I was in third grade before realizing not everyone went home to practice unicycle, gymnastics, drums, and organ after school every day. The realization blew my mind, because it was normal to me.

There were plenty of times I was frustrated by our lack of

normal in relation to other kids, but I'm philosophically able to step back and look at the bigger picture. I knew I gained as much or more than I lost in plenty of ways with our way of moving through the world. I was well aware the self-discipline our lives required was a gift for my creative free-spirited nature. My parents often said this to me. Not everyone learns to balance the two. I did. Creativity with discipline is a force to be reckoned with were words I heard more than a few times from them.

> ## Creativity with discipline is a force to be reckoned with.
> ## -Henneberryism

I applied this logic to my effort to ride a bicycle. I had a hard time learning how to ride my first bicycle. I struggled to get the hang of it, as other kids younger than me were picking up on it much faster. I had already been riding a unicycle for four years and performing in our shows for two years, so this extra wheel was in the way. It was not necessary to my little girl mind. I kept at it and tried every day collecting scratches and scrapes aplenty. It took me months and months to figure out how not to feel constricted by the second tire.

Once I had it, the victory was such a big deal my family gathered on the front porch and took pictures. My self-discipline turned toward performing tricks on my little bicycle which I preferred to ride barefoot. It was how I rode my unicycle as the first one in the line of kids to refuse to wear shoes during practice. From the earliest age I thought the more I felt the better and feeling those pedals under my feet as I gripped them with my toes made learning more sensible to me.

Making the bicycle more like my experience with my unicycle

gave me incentive to even ride this thing now, with the entirely unnecessary, as I saw it, second tire. I might as well learn some tricks. It was what I saw in our performances. Professional bicyclists balancing in unusual ways entertaining audiences. This became my immediate focus. I learned to stand on my bike, use one foot to operate it, no feet, no hands on the handlebars, riding on it sideways, all in an effort to honor that one sentence I heard as a constant drumbeat in my life. Creativity with discipline is a force to be reckoned with. That became my organic brand of normal.

I had been learning tricks on unicycle. I could ride with one foot. I could ride with my feet on the wheel. I could ride backward. I was learning how to spin in circles on one wheel. I could bend and pick things up, so why couldn't I attack the bicycle looking for ways to demonstrate skills on it, as well? My whole perspective throughout life has not been run of the mill. It morphed into an entrepreneurial spirit as a matter of personal balance and survival for my creative spirit as much as anything else.

VANILLA ON A PLAIN CONE

My radar for who would and wouldn't be a good guy to date was unsophisticated, at best, as a teenager. Imperfect would be an understatement. I liked boys I found kind, cute, smart, and friendly. Funny was a bonus. It wasn't much more complicated than that, until I found myself on a first date realizing my definition of interesting might be a bit different that how others define it.

He was a fine guy, polite, and definitely had a good heart, but one thing he did was the indicator to me we could never be together and it happened in front of the counter in an ice cream shop when I was in mid-high school. We had had little to talk about, but that's not what raised my eyebrow. It was what happened in the ice cream parlor.

I was so excited to have more than two dozen ice cream flavors to choose from at this ice cream counter on our first date and it was a treat to be able to order one of my favorites that I didn't get to enjoy very much. I chose Mint Chocolate Chip and something with a ribbon of fudge woven around candy pieces all on a sugar cone. These flavors had been around much of my life, but we'd only get to eat them for special occasions.

I waited eagerly as the boy I was with considered his options. I was curious what he could choose with so many colors and patterns in the tubs before us. There was cheesecake, different types of chocolate, fruit flavors, and countless combinations of swirls, twirls and slivers of sweetness strewn throughout all of the dairy delights.

He walked up to the counter looking at the young girl behind the counter and casually said, "Vanilla on a plain cone." I was in disbelief. With all of the possibility for flavor and new experiences in this store, this was his choice? It was so normal and I couldn't see where this could go if this was our starting point. He was a great guy, just not for me. I'm quite certain I was not his ideal partner either when all was said and done. The funny thing is in my maturity now, I adore vanilla on a plain cone. So much for my lousy, unsophisticated, inner date sorting radar as a teenager.

Growing up, I wasn't focused on trying to be like everybody else. I was focused on trying to have a sense of belonging with myself and part of having that sense of belonging to myself was to identify my values so those are always the routine, the ritual, the consistent truth I can come back to in my life. Those were and are my normal.

At two-weeks-old, I was packed up and taken on the road with my performing family. Weeks after that, I was part of a magazine article on my family's travels. The article included an image of me sleeping inside a drawer pulled out of its dresser in a hotel room, because it was the safest place they could find to put me of options available. It was my mom's resourcefulness in creating a type of bassinet to keep me safe. The journalist thought it was a good illustration of our lifestyle, so I made the magazine. That was the start of my life. I was very nearly born on the road entering the world at 7 lbs. 6 oz. the fifth of six children. In fact, I was born on my oldest sister Marg's 18th birthday. We were a big family living an unorthodox lifestyle with a father who was a junior high and high school teacher during the school year applying his masters degree in gifted education and a mother whose sole focus was her family and her church.

There are plenty of traditional 'normal' ideas in the structure of my life. However, when you grow up as a professional entertainer jumping on a unicycle at two, joining in with gymnastics at just shy of five, drums, keyboard, and trumpet to follow still in grade school mixed with my advocacy-oriented nature, the idea of 'normal' could barely get off the ground for me.

LIVING NEXT TO NORMAL

We traveled all summer from the day school got out until the day the new school year started each fall, plus many weekends and most holiday breaks. I wasn't hanging out at the houses of friends all summer to have the chance to see just how different their lives were than mine.

During the holidays, we were busy every year with entertainment jobs. By the time I was eight or nine, it was as normal as putting gas in a car for me to be pulled out of bed at two in the morning and carried to the car in the frozen night to sit bundled up in the back seat of our Country Squire wood-paneled station wagon packed to the ceiling with people and things as it pulled our equipment trailer along behind making our way to entertainment jobs. I sometimes let our destination surprise me to make a game of this common family experience.

I studied snow and ice outside of my window as the WBBM News Radio sounder came on keeping my dad awake at the wheel. Since it was on the AM band, that radio station could travel with us for hundreds even thousands of miles. At other times, we'd doze to the sound of an old time radio theater program that would fill the air in the dead of the night reminding us we weren't entirely alone on our long drives. I loved those ominous theatrical radio programs and would find myself deeply engaged in them every single time.

My mom often hummed in the front seat as my siblings jockeyed for whatever space there was depending on the musical chairs of whoever made each trip doing whatever they could to pass time in a time when the only handheld toys were yo-yo's and travel bingo. Sleeping became an acrobatic act of sibling body contortions to get comfortable relying on coats and sweaters to soften hard edges around us bumping along on the roads in a time seatbelts weren't required use. I'd glance at my older brother, Mark, from time-to-time in his rust-colored waist-length winter polyester jacket sporting a beige stripe across the chest, to watch him make impressively delicate baby feet on the frost-covered frozen window using the side of his palm and fingertips, careful not to ruin the artist paper that was a frost-covered window. There was always only one chance to get it right until the next frost or until we drove through snowier, icier conditions to be able to start the window murals over again. It was common to see legal pads full of handwritten notes my oldest brother Mick would bring along to study on our distant trips prepping for law school exams. Meanwhile, my parents might be chatting together in the front seat about having more than a million miles of road behind us in their lifetime of travel together.

A common drill on those drives was a full family performance debrief after most every show pulling out of one venue headed to another to try to perfect technique, praise a well-executed skill, call out and soothe each other about an unintended mistake, scold thoughtless sloppy execution, applaud a positive unexpected outcome, and, in essence, figure out how to make the show better next time. Sometimes it was a comforting discussion and sometimes it was not, but it was a relied upon expectation and part of my normal to learn to anticipate and keep improving myself.

Making our way down the many roads, highways, and interstates, I studied the countless houses in the distance decked out for Santa's arrival during holiday travels. The colorful lights were beautiful against newly fallen glistening snow that glowed blue and even violet at times in the moonlight. I noted how peaceful and warm each home looked wondering what is was like to do nothing at the holidays except hang around in your pajamas, eat soup, watch holiday movies, sleep in, and play. That's what I imagined was happening in every house we passed with rainbow lights spread around yards covered in snow that sparkled in the nighttime glow as if each was an individual invitation to join in on their family festivals of holiday fun. I learned very early on that normal is the normal you live.

Normal is the normal you live.

As a live and let live kind of kid, this idea suited my nature. It became clear that discipline was my normal routine and ritual in our activities was my normal, as well. My personality is creative, so I don't need an incredible amount of structure to exist happily. Some people didn't understand it. I was asked more than a few times if we were a bunch of hippies, or, more amusingly, clowns. What was the story with our odd lifestyle? Were we gypsies? Did we like doing this? Were our parents treating us right? Others found it wonderful, fascinating, full of intrigue, and adventure. There were all sorts of questions I heard from people wanting to know how you can live like this in the world that doesn't do the same thing you do actually encouraging the opposite: working against what is uncommon in you.

Rethink Challenge: Don't let limits others place on themselves turn into chains for you, too. If you hang around people who don't think THEY can do things when you show spunk, spirit, and originality, you can learn to believe you can't do those things, too. If they attempt to squash you into a place that makes them feel better about not having done more things themselves, move your life in a different direction. Normal is the normal you live. You can have more than one kind of normal in your life that speaks directly to how you want to be in the world. Some people won't like it and will actively attempt to discredit you to make their own choices more sensible in their own minds. That can contaminate your spirit and pull you back down. Pssst.... Don't let it happen.

POWER

Power is not outside of you.

THE POW IN POWER

I was only a few weeks in to my first month or two in that university setting and I won't forget his words. They were seared into my brain as you'd expect would happen with a branding iron when he whispered into my ear.

As a new university student coming in as a junior, I walked into a summer class eager to get work out of the way for a lighter load in the fall semester. The class took place four days a week on hot summer midwestern afternoons on the edge of campus in a long time communication building computer lab in the shadow of, at that time, what was bragged to be the world's tallest dormitory building next door. It was a beginner reporting class and I was eager to learn.

The problem started when I was taking a test sitting next to a guy who needed to be called out for the rancid odor of his feet which I couldn't understand because he was wearing naturally air-ventilated flip flops. But, he was just another grungy college student like many of us on a sticky summer day clicking off one more class in a condensed summer session.

As I split attention between my classroom neighbor's feet and my test, the instructor approached me while milling around the room and from the very first moment it didn't feel right. He put one hand on the back of my chair. He put the other hand on the table right next to my test. He leaned in to within an inch of my face. He whispered with his warm breath hitting my neck, "You mean on top of all the other wonderful things about you, you're left handed, too?" The red hot blush of embarrassment I felt in that moment was dwarfed only by the lingering feeling of him not moving away from me fast enough and the shrinking sense that his eyes were on me for the rest of the class period. I didn't respond to his words and I didn't even look at him the rest of that class. When I turned in my test leaving the room, he didn't acknowledge me.

I was horrified by what had happened and wondered why. Why did it happen? The first thing I did walking out of the room was to look at my clothing. I was wearing a pastel plaid smock summer dress in a light cotton with tank sleeves I'd purchased at a teen girl store in a nearby mall. As a part of the warped sense of sexual responsibility women were taught in that time, I noted my dress was well below the knee. I looked at my white pointed toe flats against my bare feet while my head spun. I was scared. Did I deserve and cause what just happened? Was I asking for something without realizing it? It was the strangest feeling of no power, plus confusion. It took my mind entirely off the issue at hand which was to pass my test.

I told my boyfriend at the time and he immediately said, "What did you do to cause it?" That didn't help. Despite my self-questioning to find solid ground for my mind, I knew I did not cause this. He echoed a tired refrain we hear as women all too often. The puzzle of it was at the surface in the shallow pool of life many people skim along in without questioning it. I didn't live there. I lived in a deeper place already with no idea what to do with the way I worked. I realized this boyfriend didn't get it.

Eventually, I realized I was overqualified for the relationship, as that boyfriend wasn't ready for me yet like so many learn about relationship dynamics on their way through life. When it came to my instructor, I thought maybe it was a one-time deal and I tried to put it aside. I ignored it hoping it wouldn't happen again and he'd get his sense back, but that didn't happen.

I began to dread going to class as he gave me more attention than others, called out my answers as the strongest ones when I gave them even if I knew I wasn't breaking intellectual ground with my work in this classroom.

One day, he was shopping on the other side of one of the college bookstores when I was running errands. I felt him plant his eyes on me. He didn't stop watching me as I moved around the store getting what I came for, a couple of cards, a pen, and a piece of chocolate. His staring was blatant, creepy, and seemed ridiculous. He was twice my age, married, and it was getting more frightening for me.

I watched him walking down the hallways at school yukking it up with people who ran the department. In fact, the department chair and he were seemingly good friends which added to my feeling of being trapped as I was a brand new student in the department.

My hope was if I could just get out of his class, if I could survive his class, I could put what this gross scene was behind me.

One day leaving the classroom, as we handed in our work he stopped me and said, "You should stop by my office some time," which I did not want to do. I knew better. My intuition told me if there is ever a time to not do something, this is it.

I asked around. A few people confirmed what I wondered. He was squirrelly. I, frankly, wasn't experienced enough in life at that point to ask particularly seamy questions about what he might be after or doing with students he handpicked to give his intimidating attention. All I knew was this was awful. He was friends with leaders in the department. I knew I wanted this major. What was I going to do?

My dodging his requests to go to his office turned into him saying that I didn't deserve a good grade in the class, because I wouldn't do what he said. He told me, "You should take me out for a coke." I blew it off and he kept bringing it up until I felt like I was in an even bigger bind.

By this time - I was at wit's end. This is not how I wanted to start my career in journalism in my first class at university level making this my first topic of conversation with leadership. I'd already heard plenty of dismissing and shaming things over the years about women keeping themselves in line, asking for poor behavior they received from men. It's often what we learn as women and, no, that doesn't always source from our parents. My parents would be have horrified to hear what I was dealing with and they would have likely had a spirited face-to-face with that instructor, but I didn't want that. I wasn't looking for a police report. I wasn't looking for a court case. I wasn't looking for a street fight. I was looking for a career. I wanted a chance.

> I wasn't looking for a police report. I wasn't looking for a court case. I wasn't looking for a street fight. I was looking for a career. I wanted a chance.

In my desperation to find a solution, I told my older sister who was a teenager when I was born and had her own experiences with this realm of life. Mary Zita sat me down and strategized with me. Her first words were, "He doesn't think you have any power. He doesn't think you have any support network around you and he's preying on that. Here's what you do," She said. She told me to tell him I have family in town and at the university, in fact. Plus, she said to make sure he knows I have a brother who is an attorney. She said, "Have the coke with him in a public place and toss all of this in to let him know you aren't weak and lonely here. You aren't desperate."

I did just that and he did back off, in part, because class ended and I ducked him every time I saw him around the building that year. I made myself unavailable. I avoided signing up for his classes and anything he was a faculty advisor for as I was still unsure if I was the only one he did this to. I just didn't get it. You know you aren't asking for it, but there is apparently something about you that triggers this in him I remember thinking at the time, but not fully understanding. I cringed every time I saw him buddy up to leadership in the hallways.

The next semester after having avoided him for a few months, I walked into the class of another instructor a few minutes early and this squirrelly one was there gathering up his things having taught the class right before mine. He was talking to my instructor as I walked in the room. Once he saw me, he walked over to me talking to that instructor the whole time moving from their topic to telling him I was so wonderful and one of his favorite students. Without pausing, he put his arms around me in a full body embrace and lifted me off the ground in a tight nuzzling bear hug. My body went stiff and my arms were pasted to my sides. I said nothing…no words - nothing. I'd just been violated in this angering way and I could say nothing as I watched the other instructor act like it was no big deal and continue to unpack his supplies for class as more students filed in.

This problem professor had a habit of calling me out in the hallway if I didn't duck out of view. I didn't know what to do about it.

Then, I saw it. I saw a flyer on the wall. A woman was coming to campus to talk about sexual harassment in the workplace in a meeting room at our student center. I didn't know a lot about sexual harassment, but I knew enough to feel sure I was dealing with this very thing. I wanted to know if this workplace topic was different than what you experience in a college. I wasn't getting paid to be here. I was paying to be here, so I wondered if I had to accept what was handed to me since I was choosing to be in this place. Or, maybe I had even more clout not to accept it. I wanted it to stop. I didn't feel I had power.

I wanted it to stop. I didn't feel I had power.

The room at the student center that day was busy. Many people turned out, but not so many I would not be heard. I went for my own information, but could not believe my eyes when this Professor Squirrel walked in to listen to this woman's talk about sexual harassment in the workplace, too.

I placed myself by a wood railing with wrought iron posts where I could easily be seen, so I'd have a shot at asking a question listening intently, as she spoke, for anything that could help me navigate this frustration. It was all so workplace-focused, I wasn't sure I had a case to make in the communication department of a public university. That's how little was understood about the insidious problem of sexual harassment at that time.

As she finished and was ready to take questions I decided to lay out my scenario as if it were a workplace to see what she would say to that. Maybe that would tell me what I needed to know. The squirrel would be there to hear it and maybe he'd get the message. I wasn't in a situation I felt I could or would be heard. I wanted help with no idea how to get it. I needed to feel safe in this school till I graduated and this was my best idea.

When she noticed my hand in the air, she called for my question. I laid out the scenario in a hypothetical. "Let's say you are on a team of people in the workplace and you continue to get singled out with whispers in your ear, comments of meeting with your boss alone to get and give special attention," On and on I went explaining. At the end, she stammered answering me. I could tell my thin veil of 'what if' was, likely, ineffective as my specifics clearly spoke to something. She said, "That does sound like sexual harassment."

I felt vindicated. I wanted to have a way to name it and know it was what it felt like. It was a discombobulating violation. It was a power play. It was a game and I wasn't given the rules. I could not win and didn't want to. I just wanted a career one day.

The Professor Squirrel's eyes were on me as I asked the question and when the speaker started to answer, I could still feel out of the corner of my eye his eyes still on me. She was answering and he was watching me. I was now satisfied knowing the way he watched and paid attention told me he knew I was talking about him. And, he did, if not from the lingering eyes, from what happened the next time I saw him.

The next time I saw him was in the building where this whole episode began my first days at the university and he stopped me. I'll never forget any of it. It was all so emotionally draining and frustrating for me, yet headed toward a beautiful outcome in it's own way. I even remember the spot it happened in the long white hallway between classrooms.

He started to talk quietly and sweetly, "Hey," He said looking down not making eye contact, "You know the other day at that talk?" He paused for a moment and then continued, "You weren't talking about me, were you?"

I looked at him as a big smile of personal confidence and power replaced the fear I'd felt in that building for months. I said in an exaggeratedly confused direct tone, "What on earth would make YOU think I was talking about YOU?" I looked him directly in the eye and let the pause hang there a while, before I turned and trotted away leaving him standing in the hallway still looking at me.

After that, I didn't even care if I bumped into him anymore, because I felt a new power. I'd been validated by a woman who had no idea she'd validated me, in his presence. It happened against a backdrop of others with no clue why this student was talking so specifically about a hypothetical workplace situation she wasn't even old enough to have yet. But, I did have it, in a classroom, many times, with no clue how to change it until I did.

He knew. I knew. It was over. I had my power back.

VOICE CAN BE JUSTICE ENOUGH

Justice can be elusive. Some might think he should've been taken to task legally. Confronting the person who hurt me in a way that gave me my power back worked for me in that time. I had no specific knowledge of anyone else he might've been treating the way he was treating me. I'd only been told by a couple other students he had a squirrelly nature. If I had heard any specific evidence, it would've been a no-brainer, because I wouldn't have been entirely alone facing it. I had no template, departmental sisterhood, or strong sense of community in this college environment yet to do anything else about it, I was so new. What I did felt powerful at the time for me.

Classically, we view power as outside of us. It is something to be attained and is in the distance. Hearing the word power, our starting point is not usually thinking of it as what is inside of us. This is a shift in perspective that benefits forward movement when facing difficult times.

Would I handle it differently in a different time? It's hard to say, but knowing what I know now the conversation would be received more readily and words of one college female have a better chance of being believed now and that's still not even certain. I do believe shame lives in silence and telling our stories is the best place to start, however imperfect our approach might be to our solutions.

> I do believe shame lives in silence and telling our stories is the best place to start, however imperfect our approach might be to our solutions.

If it were happening to a young woman I know today, in addition to talking to a trusted family member, I'd suggest she log her experiences as specifically as possible including dates. I'd tell her to find the Women's Studies department where she could likely find thoughtful ears and possible guidance to navigate the situation in an academic environment. It's merely what I would have done knowing what I know now. I'd have been focused on finding a group of people who could possibly be open to my story before I did anything else.

Just the idea that presenting women's experiences under a branded name #MeToo is a key to being taken seriously says a lot. Why do we have to stand in a group and slap a logo on it to be heard? Our words, historically, haven't been received as valid on their own way too often - one woman - one experience at a time. The word systemic is key in the answer. It's a rare personal story that can drown out the noise of an engrained cultural habit. We have built lifetimes of stories on certain ideas we rely on for predictability and perceived safety in our marriages, families, friendships, workplaces, movies, marketing campaigns, and music industries to name a few. When people construct the foundation of their lives on certain ideas, crumbling those ideas with earth-shaking new ways of thinking is hard. But get this: people do it. It can be outrageously painful to move the needle. It requires us to look inside ourselves for answers.

If women are only viewed as lover or mother versus multi-dimensional human being with agency respected for her individual voice and vital role in building a better world, we're in trouble. Some people are heavily invested in status quo. It's as if you challenge their self-worth when you lack reverence for sameness. This idea undermines personal power, because it champions status quo and keeping peace over personal autonomy. It's a dangerous slide. The battle for better treatment becomes less about what's actually happening and more about protecting comfort zones.

In recent months, one thoughtful professional woman told me she understands women having one case of sexual misconduct behind them, but 20? 30? Then she thinks the woman is the problem. The word systemic isn't in her thinking. Wildly disheartening.

I'm like so many women with my 30+ stories of varying degrees of mistreatment. So many of us can say with confidence it's systemic and corrosion of the spirit can be hard to remedy no matter how smart, wise, aware, connected, capable, resilient, and seemingly prepared you are at overcoming what is before you.

The #MeToo movement was key to my own realization that when I was grabbed, hugged, and/or kissed against my will, that was sexual assault. I'd been raped at the end of college by someone

I didn't know which I discuss at length in the later chapter called Worth. I'm well aware of the wide range of experiences under this umbrella. Given my personal experience and, as distinctive as each perspective is, there have been commonalities in all of it. I wasn't a bad sport for not playing along in any of them. No wonder I've gone through the internal psychological processes I have in these situations. I was a conscious person walking into my career fully aware of what was ahead and I was still a frog in a pot of water heating up so to speak.

You can't anticipate all outrageous behavior before it happens when it's not how you treat people. That's an anxiety-provoking standard to expect of women.

You can't anticipate all outrageous behavior before it happens when it's not how you treat people. That's an anxiety-provoking standard to expect of women. I saw sexual harassment as a pesky frustration and something for me to personally overcome hoping it didn't impact my career and reputation - merely an occupational hazard. It's warped and how way too many of us are conditioned in career. We learned to deal with it.

It became so pervasive that learning to navigate around it, avoid it, challenge it, call it out, and diffuse it has been as vital a skill set in my work life as anything else - likely more important because it keeps women safe and alive. The most significant impact of absorbing this kind of negative disempowering treatment is that my personal attention to myself splintered in college. While men around me could focus on their career and personal desires, I had the added weight of anticipating all scenarios that could jeopardize my reputation, career, and safety while at the same time knowing what I looked like mattered in a way that built and reduced my power all at once. It's an incredibly frustrating no-win situation, unless you play along for as long as you can knowing you will inevitably lose at the end because sexual harassment and sexual assault are not set ups for professional success. Playing along for the sake of career climbing is not how I'm made, so I protected myself in as many ways as I could over the years and built my career on as much professional independence as I could knowing I had no interest in compromising myself, so taking control of my destiny was the only way to combat it.

Human dignity has to stay central if we survive as a culture. Kindness and decency are huge components. It seems like a no-brainer. Much of this solution is about drawing a line and requiring colleagues to grow up and understand they have power to stop this by not playing along. This is a collective effort. We impact each other.

Plenty of women prey on male weakness and it has to be called out, too. Make no mistake. Let's show them they don't need to reduce themselves with this phantom power and, phantom it is, because there's little to no lasting substance in it. It hurts all of us.

In our positions of power, we hold great responsibility to get this right and demand human dignity be respected. Power is about each individual's right to be seen fully as who they are, not power as something to hoard and revere only for what it soaks up and consumes. In all of this is an excellent opportunity to commit to doing right by each other. Remember this: Internal power gives you trajectory. External power gives you responsibility.

Internal power gives you trajectory.
External power gives you responsibility.

There are times when any personal power you felt you had is lost in circumstances you felt were out of your control and you're left picking up pieces with no idea how to carry on. I've realized something sitting with this very question of what to do when you feel smashed by adversity in life with no personal power. There are times you feel everything you've built your life around appears to be crumbling and you sit in the middle of it with no more ideas.

Having nothing to lose is a gift in redefining power and it's often hard won through immense pain. You know what it is to be hurt, shredded, and disappointed enough to feel you have nothing to lose anymore. When you no longer fear failing - what is there to fear? Nothing.

You now have a superpower. You know that no matter what you just keep breathing and go on one step at a time one day at a time. When this idea sinks in - you can choose to become a force to be reckoned with - as a deep, unshakable inner strength can take hold.

You are off the grid of mainstream expectation.
You no longer fit the cookie cutter mold.
You've shaken free from status quo.
You are not an ant marching.
You are not a lemming.
You're wide awake - aware you're a blank canvas.
The picture of life you now paint is all you.
It's liberating - if you allow it.

You now have an opportunity. You get to follow your own heart and create a life that speaks to your own core values - no one else's. You get to decide what your life means to you. You get to just... Be... You.

Rethink Challenge: Can you view power as something that starts inside of you rather than something you seek

approval for from outside of yourself? Power is you, but your challenge is to recognize what that means to you and how you can go forward in your life making decisions that speak to that energetic force. Along the way - try to be kind and compassionate with yourself - as others benefit by association. Congratulations.

REGRET

Regret is less difficult when you know your reasons why.

BE YOUR OWN CHEERING SECTION

Upon transferring to the university, one of my first decisions was to find cheerleading tryouts and run with it. However, at this same time I'd been watching friends battle conscious and unconscious eating disorders and I was slipping into the same patterns. For some, it was rigid eating. I remember one academic standout in my friend circle battling anorexia declaring how full she was after having begged to get down to supper in the cafeteria and how we weren't moving fast enough for her. Once we were there only beginning to dig in, there was a collective pause in conversation when she said within a minute or two of sitting down with her tray how incredibly full she was having consumed exactly only one half of one canned peach. She was one of the university's top collegiate scholars at that time. I had another friend who lived on diet pop and cigarettes during the week, so she felt she could drink alcohol without caloric regret on the weekends. She lived on cigarettes and diet pop for days at a time. Think about that. I'm talking about amazing young women as I think back on that time. Here's how the idea of regret impacted me. I went through the workshops to prepare for tryouts for the university cheerleading squad and was doing amazingly well. I was already a gymnast, had a performance background, and 7-8 years of cheerleading behind me including two stints as Captain. I was the first of the tryout group to achieve one of the required lifts and I was solid on the required skills. I knew by the end of the practices the day before tryouts I had the technical skills to make the squad. But, I didn't try out. I blew off the big day. I didn't go. I sat in my dorm room and thought about what I was doing as tryouts went on. In fact, when it was over and judges posted who made it as promised, I went across the street from my dorm where they posted the list to see who made the squad. I was happy for them and sad for me, but also didn't feel I had a choice. The next year another cheerleader from my former college squad made it on that same university cheerleading team adding to my confidence I could have, very possibly, made that happen. Did I regret it? I'll get to that.

Here's what I knew about myself and my reality at the time. I had an eating disorder. It wasn't debilitating, but it was a nagging force in my life. As I mentioned, I was surrounded by young women in my social circle struggling with similar issues. I knew I wasn't in a good place with personal versus external expectation at that time. When university cheerleading leadership said there would be daily weigh-ins and we'd be reprimanded with additional exercise requirements if we were over expectation by even a scant pound or three, I knew I was doomed. I knew I'd fail because my weight fluctuated by 5 pounds up and down when I was super healthy based on any number of standard reasons. But, add to that this disordered eating pattern and my heart sank.

This was at a time when being weighed meant simply stand on a scale. We aren't talking about sophisticated machinery capable of reading water weight and body mass index. I was afraid the pressure would add to this disordered eating issue I was trying to solve on my own, not make it better by encouraging me to seek even more kudos outside myself. I didn't have the tools to fix what I was dealing with. My intuition told me that university cheerleading squad would not be a healthy choice for me particularly at that time. I made the bittersweet decision to beg off, but having proved to myself with my accomplishments in the workshops that I was as skilled and more skilled than others and could have made that squad. Sometimes that kind of awareness is enough.

I had been a cheerleader throughout junior high, high school and at my community college. In fact, I restarted the cheerleading squad at my community college looking for new activities in that environment and having blown dust off a box of old cheerleading uniforms that were aging in some forgotten corner of some closet.

My approach to life is to take the bull by the horns and make something happen. I feel alive doing it, I love giving people a hand in making their desires happen, and I enjoy lifting people up. Plus, I appreciated the athleticism gymnastics added to cheerleading. But, considering all of that, life doesn't always have to be predictable to work out amazingly well. Sometimes chance and unpredictability take you on entirely new adventures that are better than you would have been able to dream up or strategically plan all by yourself.

CHEER FOR CONSCIOUS DECISIONS

Some people would like to tell someone like me in that cheerleading tryout situation I was a quitter. We spend a lot of time in this culture acquiring experiences merely to keep from having to say we regret not doing it later - that we are not quitters. We walk over people, situations, and even ourselves to take all of the life we can out of the air and call it ours to make sure we keep that evil word regret at bay. Our accomplishment warps into being about the accomplishment itself more than it does about our grasp of enough and that what is best for us could actually be leaving space for qualified others who also might want to experience something on the path, too, and might be more equipped at this moment for it.

There is a harmony in the idea we don't always make the right choices, but when we know why we make the choices we do, regrets are fewer because we paid attention to our reasons at that time. When you pay attention to yourself walking through difficult decisions, peace can come more easily on the other side. I believed that at 18 and I believe it now.

When you pay attention to yourself walking through difficult decisions, peace can come more easily on the other side.

I'm decades past disordered eating grounded in who I am, so this memory is distant now. Did I regret not trying out that day? No and is that a regret? Yes, but it's not a brutal all-consuming 'when there's a will there's a way; regret. I was learning self-mastery at that time using my personal boundary learning process to make decisions for myself. I was learning to stand ground for myself the best way I knew how at the time. I was learning to be a grown up. However unusual, I was standing up for myself the best way I knew how. Plus, I was embarrassed. No one knew what I was dealing with. That's not something to regret. Do I regret all of the fun of that squad? In some ways, I did for a few years. I also knew if I found myself hyper-focused on food, my weight, and weigh-ins, these relationships would be built on something I didn't think would be healthy for me in the long run.

Regret is something I think about quite a bit. It's a now you see it now you don't hide and seek idea to me. When things are great, a person often wouldn't change a thing. When things are bad, a person is more likely to feel regrets aplenty. You can be solid and centered and confident and happy as can be and still have regrets. I've given many talks over the years in my career and one thing that comes up often is living with no regrets. People want that life. They would talk to me about wanting to check things off the list to keep regret away. I'm not all that different. I'm not looking for reasons to feel rotten. One of my mantras has always been, if you make conscious decisions, there are fewer regrets because you, at least, know why you made decisions you did. There's comfort in awareness. I think I was making an effort to be deliberate all the way back in diapers. It's how I work.

Some people have sworn to me they have not one regret. They are certain of their path. My eyebrow raises when I hear that, because it doesn't seem to take into account how we impact others. There is hardly any way I can imagine I haven't hurt people along the way as I was learning and working my way along the path as much as I would hope not to have done that. I would and do regret those moments. I care about people and wouldn't want to think I caused anyone unnecessary pain.

When you live a life with a patchwork of experiences sometimes sewn together well and sometimes with gaping holes as you try new things, adjust, crash, rebuild, triumph, redirect, it's a disservice to yourself to think there'll be no regrets. The amount of control or thoughtlessness I'd have had to live with to have no regrets isn't in me. I'd be pretty boring to be around, too, because I'd limit my experiences to avoid that dreaded word's impact on my life. Most things have a light and dark side.

Most things have a light and dark side.

Along the way, I learned to mellow the heck out, trust the process, trust my ability to overcome, stop externalizing my value, and keep moving forward - so regrets weren't as scary. I had to know I'd be ok and that there were numerous possible outcomes I was capable of coping with and achieving for a well-lived, adventurous life.

A key way to diminish unnecessary regrets is in how you communicate when someone is being rude, mean-spirited, or confrontational in a toxic way. Whether or not I feel badly about that outcome depends on how solid and centered I feel given stress and general responsibilities.

When I'm solid and centered, what I do and say comes from a thoughtful deliberate place, so I'm pretty unshakable. When I'm scattered, I'm more likely to let it bother me as I question myself wondering if I was off-base.

When you're kind and assertive able to call out something to keep a conversation open with the goal of fostering more supportive mutual understanding, some people do not like it. It's as if they're threatened by your openness. Maybe some people get used to living in a passive aggressive or avoidant way, so direct communication feels much too vulnerable. You learn about people when they are rude. There is real value in seeking first to understand while not apologizing to yourself or anyone else for holding ground on your own behalf. You owe that to yourself.

It's disheartening, because this result shines a light on a bigger picture issue about how we often communicate in the collective conversation. Nobody has to win any discussions. We can seek to understand one another with compassion graciously helping each other along. It doesn't have to get complicated. Be the change makes a lot of sense and part of that change is learning to be with regret, so you don't allow yourself to crumble under it's weight. It makes space for your humanness.

Rethink Challenge: There are few, if any, real regrets when we require ourselves to know why we make the decisions we do. When we know that, we understand who we are and where we were in our lives at the time of a potential opportunity or pivotal moment. No one can be fully aware and all knowing all places all the time every single day of their lives. It's an absurd idea.

TRUST

*Trusting others starts with trusting
yourself to persevere.*

TEENAGE TEACHER

I was only a few months into my first year in college when I was called to a counseling office and asked an unexpected question. Would I be willing to be the choir teacher for a small parochial school about 10 minutes away from my college for the fall semester. The full-time music teacher was taking a leave of absence and school administrators needed someone willing to take on regular music classes and prepare the students Kindergarten through eighth grade for their Christmas concert.

I had no idea how to do that. I was not a teacher. I was an 18-year-old freshman in college being asked to handle an entire school's worth of children to get them ready for a holiday concert. God is a big deal in a parochial school and when you sing the old standards, you don't want to mess anything up. People know exactly how those are supposed to sound. The expectation seemed high. It would actually happen in the huge church next door to the school. The students would stand on risers at the front altar-level during Advent, a significant holy time during the church calendar year. The kids singing to their parents was, in essence, a Christmas present. Who doesn't love seeing their kindergarten, first, second, third, fourth, fifth, all with through eighth-grade child singing holiday favorites while decked out in red, green, and white all together in perfect harmony at the front of their church feeling wonder of the season?

I wasn't sure I could do it. I mulled it over and thought about how much music I'd been surrounded by in my life up to that point. I'd been playing multiple instruments with my family's stage shows. I sang through high school and junior high and had been in numerous contests. I knew how the system worked. I was still fresh off high school, even if this was elementary and junior high level. What if I screwed up? What if they didn't respond to me? What if they didn't like me? What if they rejected me? What if I embarrassed myself?

I knew what I had to do in my fear. When I fear something that's generally the exact direction I move to face myself and get better. I said yes.

Within a few days, I was walking into the building feeling the nostalgia of the building in the walls. The dark brick walls, the white tiled floors, and echoes in the hallways of various lessons being taught in classrooms. Stepping into the music room, I moved my eyes around the room slowly. It looked like a comfortable place to be with all of these new students. The old upright piano stood encased in dark wood and seemed to command ownership in the space sitting to my left. The surroundings were simple, but functional and my first decision was to sit down at the piano and play a little to get a feel for this space and find the sense of belonging I was searching for there. I went through some of the holiday music we would be playing O Little Town of Bethlehem, Up On The Housetop, Jingle Bells and I began to feel at home. So far, so good.

NEW DAY NEW CHALLENGES

When the first class filed in, I found myself helping make them comfortable with me instead of the other way around. They were first graders and first graders are adorable. My day took off and I enjoyed this entirely new experience, because I walked into it with the idea I'll give it what I have and see how it works out. That's all I can ask of myself.

I taught there every week through autumn weather going through the music over and over. Of all of the instruments to know respectably well attempting to become an instant choir teacher, being able to cope with a piano was incredibility useful. I'd been playing keyboard for years having taken lessons on a Hammond organ since I was seven. Piano is different. I had only recently started teaching myself how to play bass clef. Bass clef is a huge part of playing piano. Between classes at my nearby college, I'd sneak into the dark auditorium between classes to teach myself how to play treble and bass clef together, not the easiest effort when you've basically ignored the lower rung of notes for a decade.

I was taught to play organ in an unorthodox way as my parents' interest in having all of us kids learn to play keyboard was to be able to play for random entertainment acts who joined in the shows we were part of. My siblings and I were, generally, the band for those productions. We were taught to get up and running fast by learning to build chords. That way no matter how a piece of music looked that was set in front of us from whatever corner of the world and it was, indeed, from everywhere, we could decipher it with our understanding of chords. In fact, some music only had guitar chords on it and, given how we learned, we could make music of it on keyboard, trumpet, and drums - the instruments in our family band. We were each skilled on something and most of us were interchangeable on several shining a bit brighter on instruments we each took to more easily.

There was a rag tag quality to our ability to turn random wrinkled sheets of music in various languages and pen scratches into the sounds that drove an entire production as we practiced before performances. We had a deep list of our own music to use as substitutes should a performer have no preference or theirs was plain indecipherable as would happen from time to time.

I was not a trained musician in terms of formal college education. My music background consisted of my family's expectation I know how to play in professional settings backed up by private lessons. I practiced a half hour on the drums every day from the time I was five until I was a teenager. I practiced a half hour a day on our Hammond organs from age seven when my fingers could still not even span an octave until I was in my mid-teens when I could do that with ease. My regular trumpet practicing coincided with my school band starting at age 10.

We'd also walk into the house over the years and find new instruments our parents would come across in their adventures and we'd be asked to figure out how to learn them. I distinctly remember a day as a teenager when I came home to find dozens of bells at my house my dad had found somewhere and polished up. We no sooner had one set of bells than we had another. There were hanging bells and hand bells now and we were told dad had booked my brother and I into a large fair with three performances a day during all of the days of the fair. Our job? Learn them and perform well once we got there. It was nerve-racking, adventurous, maddening, fascinating, and our version of normal. My brother and I pulled it off and sounded like we understood bells. It's a good example of the world I grew up in with my sisters and brothers. I wasn't afraid to dive in to a new experience.

Between general studies classes in college, what I understood about holiday music in my brand new role as a teenage parochial school choir K-8 teacher was the lovely thing about standards is they don't change. This traditional music is constructed with simple melodies. It was a staple in our family music performance set lists. This could not be any more difficult than sitting on stage a couple of hours before a big production having someone hand us music from Bulgaria we could not read. I knew deep down I could do this music teacher thing.

Plus, a lot of holiday music is constructed with simple chords so I could sing and play piano. This starting point made it, at least, possible. Discipline in the classroom? I'd have to wing it walking into the middle of so many different aged kids I didn't know. I pulled a girlfriend in to help me and we did it.

I prepared an entire K-8 parochial school for their Christmas concert my freshman year college over a couple of months time.

On the day of the concert, all of the students filed up to the front standing on risers at the altar. Greenery and holiday decorations were everywhere given the time of year in rich reds and greens and purples. Twelve large ornate lantern style lights hung on chains from the ceiling. Sixteen marble pillars on each side of us held up a ceiling so high, the echo of the children's voices sounded angelic. When it was over, I was given a standing ovation and school leaders gave me a gift. It was a pretty gold bracelet that I wore proudly. It was the nicest piece of jewelry I'd ever owned to that point. I was no longer a parochial school choir teacher anymore, but I was proud of one thing that took me there. I trusted that no matter what happened, I would be ok in the end. I was petrified and unqualified in a formal sense walking in, but I trusted my ability to still be standing at the end no matter the outcome. If they hated me, rejected me, and I was miserable, I decided I'd still learn something and would have at least tried to help.

TRUST YOURSELF FIRST

To a good extent, trusting others is actually about trusting yourself. Do you trust your own ability to stand up, brush yourself off, and move on if things don't work out as you'd like. Yeah...I know. There's no justice in it if you risk trust and it doesn't work out when your heart is true in what you pursue.

Often our fear of trusting others is, in part, about our inability to trust our own strength to reinvent should that be the sensible path after adversity; whatever the brand.

You can hope people will keep their word. You can hope they'll operate the way you would. You can hope you share mutual values when they sound aligned in your talks together.

The thing is actions speak louder than words and humans do what humans do. They make poor choices sometimes, make mistakes, and sometimes it hurts you - badly.

When you've been lied to, often the lying is beyond you. The person lying has a more primary concern in what I've learned. They lied to themselves on the way to hurting you. You can't fix that. That's work they have to do. They won't change without facing themselves. If none of what this person shares as who they are actually is what you were led to believe, you have to trust your own resilience. Expecting too much can send you down the path of controlling behavior and that's no fun for anyone.

Expecting too much can send you down the path of controlling behavior and that's no fun for anyone.

A common dilemma: how do you allow yourself to trust people again after being hurt to get back a spark for life? There is self trust in trusting other people. I learned to tackle this with radical positivity. I inundate myself with good stuff. I make growing the good in my life my full-time job. I dive in to all the reading material I can find on topics I want more of in my life. I realized early on creativity, having a playful adventurous spirit, optimism, self-compassion, and heart wisdom were the path out of my darkness. But, I had to relentlessly not allow anything to contaminate that inner knowing.

Part of what you're hurt by can be your own inability to have avoided the scene you now find yourself in, despite your best efforts. It's an unfair thing to do to yourself, but we do it anyway sometimes when we dare to care. When working your way back to center, see innovation as the goal and a way of life. If the noise I hear outside of myself tells me I cannot, I block it. When you hurt deeply, you're already swimming in enough tough stuff. You don't need pile on no matter how much someone thinks they're helping you telling you the way it looks from their vantage point. If they haven't worked on their own stuff, you can find yourself holding their residue. Have your own back best you can.

Bad stuff can smash your joy. Find the way back from those experiences by focusing on the positive and refusing to get sucked into the undertow of negativity. Be good to people, but start with yourself.

Trusting yourself and your ability to persevere enough that you can experience the free fall of not knowing and let it be the uncertain experience it is without allowing it to destroy your spirit in the process. Being hurled into the great abyss of ambiguity is so often incredibly anxiety-provoking.

Here's an idea known to make brains hurt. We have very little, if any, control of much of anything. We build tidy mental and physical frameworks around ourselves to set up a type of safety perimeter. It makes sense because it appears to tame the chaos around us until tough stuff happens reminding us how little control we have over so very many things.

Do you believe you can be ok and find joy, laughter, and stay in touch with yourself if the ambiguity never goes away? You might as well.

Rethink Challenge: Your challenge with the word trust is to trust yourself. We think of trust as outward facing, but what if it's more of an inward knowing about ourselves that gives this word it's most useful meaning. Can you trust yourself to be ok no matter what life deals you? That is your rethink challenge in learning to trust yourself - having your own back and knowing you will be ok no matter what happen.

WORTH

*Worth is your birthright and not
owned by external forces.*

ALL NIGHT IN THE DARK

*Sitting silently in my own car on a country dirt and grass path in
an unfamiliar place in the dark a couple miles outside one of my
midwestern home area's largest small towns of about 14,000 residents,
I dared not make a sound. It was finally over. He had climbed over
the console and back to the driver's side of my car as my Yaz Upstairs
at Eric's cassette finished playing softly in the background.*

*I sat overwhelmed in the passenger seat with a bruised feeling
on the sides of each knee from pressure where he used his legs to pin
one against the door and the other against the console to control my
movement. He'd been a football player at a bigger school and was
much stronger than me. I could still feel his dark scratchy pullover
sweater against my skin and knew I would not forget his acid-washed
baggy blue jeans and caramel brown dress shoes with two tassels on*

each of them. In fact a couple hours away on my college campus in the following months, I shuddered whenever I saw those kinds of jeans or shoes walking toward me. There were countless unassuming stars sparkling overhead on that cold Illinois night. It was Black Friday.

I'd given him my keys as part of a group of us deciding to head together to someone's house. Everyone left at the same time and he and I ended up alone in my car with the destination house only blocks away. As cars pulled out together, he told me he wanted to show me something on the way detouring from the group. I was confused and asked why. He accelerated my car to 90 mph angry and mumbling about having been dissed earlier that night by a former female college classmate of mine I distantly knew to be a kind young woman as I yelled for him to stop. He slowed my car eventually turning down a dark path. What he showed me was a new level of evil at the edge of town.

He stopped the car next to railroad tracks and attacked me despite my tears begging for him to stop. He did not stop. My screams and cries were met with answers that I was pretty, cute, and he liked me, not the response I wanted. What I wanted was for this stranger to stop what he was doing, get off of me, and let me go. This was before cell phones, GPS, and social media. Nobody knew where we were.

Within minutes of climbing off of me, he was sleeping in the driver's seat with my keys in his possession. Paralyzed with fear, tears on my face, yet savoring silence and being able to move now with him off my body. If I opened the door, the light and noise of the door would wake him and I didn't want him any angrier. If I ran, I knew my car was a weapon and I didn't want him chasing me down. I saw no place to hide. I was nowhere. This silence in the dead of the night was the only safety I had for the moment and it was enough however long it lasted. He kept me out there all night and, for those hours, I didn't dare move or make a sound believing it was my safest choice. I even controlled my breath to make sure I couldn't hear myself breathing, I was so afraid he might wake up and hurt me again.

You feel used up after rape. It's shredding, confusing, and traumatic. It was a chilly night the day after Thanksgiving 1990 when this happened to me and I had only met that college guy that night trusting he was an okay person, because of all of the people we were around treating him like he was their friend.

Once home, I collapsed inside the door on my childhood living room floor curling up in the fetal position in front of the fireplace under the high-ceilings of our big old white three-story house. My parents were angry and distressed that they didn't know where I was as it wasn't my nature to stay out all night at parties. As they picked up on the tone of what was happening, the frustration and anger turned toward this faceless person as I hugged my black tights-covered legs over the Queen Anne's Lace floral pattern of the knee-length skorts I'd worn all night. I was lying on my side in my favorite black high-collar long sleeve button down blouse. It still had an antique broach pinned over the top button. I cried as I hugged myself on our green carpeted front room floor. I'd never done that before and my parents were shocked at the scene unfolding before them.

I watched my dad rage and I watched my mom soften as she went emotionally internal in their mutual uncertainty as to how to handle this kind of moment. They called my oldest sister, Marg, for guidance and the chaos turned into a plan of action when they, ultimately, took me to an emergency room she was familiar with an hour away.

My mom sat on the stairs of our house in her nightgown and wrung her hands in sadness, as the story unfolded. My dad blamed my car which was a 1987 black Camaro, a car he and I loved dearly. He blamed me for handing over my keys. He blamed my going out that night. He blamed my sister for pushing me to go out that night. He blamed the guy and wanted to find him. My dad blamed himself.

With my mom by my side, I was informed at the hospital that if they were going to treat me for rape I was required to file a police report at which point the ordeal was entirely out of my hands. My immediate thoughts were, "Now, I'll be a court case." "I have to see him again?" "I have to talk to him again?" "I have to relive this on a witness stand?" "People will know about this?" "Is this my fault?" "How will this impact my reputation I've worked hard to protect?" "How will this affect my career and ability to get a job?" "Will I seem difficult, a liability, and too much trouble for potential employers if this gets out?" "People will try to say I wanted this and that I caused it so they can protect him." "Will this ordeal make me look weak to people when they find out?" "If he was capable of this, what else if he capable of doing to me or my family?" "Is this my fault?" "Is this my fault?" "Is this my fault?"

I was already afraid and all of this new uncertainty added an extra layer of fear when hours before I thought I was celebrating a run-of-the-mill birthday for some kid I didn't know. The rape kit required a police report. Without the ability to mentally process that fast, I said I wasn't ready for all of that. They told me my chart would indicate I was treated for a 'bronchial infection' instead assuring me they'd still check my general health as if I'd been raped without the more detailed and invasive evidence collection of a rape kit. I had no idea what I was avoiding. My focus was on safeguarding this final remnant of privacy when so much of my inexperienced intimate life had already been compromised. It was the tiny bit of control I felt I still had in my state of shock.

The process included a handful of pills I dutifully took without even asking why. Sadly, as the nurse held out her hand to me with a collection of various-sized capsules and tablets in earthen colors, she told me she, too, had been raped. For her, it was when she was 18. She said it was upsetting, but is just the way it is and shrugged telling me I wasn't alone. I was sad and enraged by this club I had been initiated into with no desire for membership. How could this be behavior women have to accept? I could make no sense of it, but had no strength to find answers in the moment.

I was also given precautionary medicine for chlamydia, in case it popped up later. Medical staff told me I didn't seem to have it, but they didn't want to take chances informing me it could severely damage my reproductive system if it showed up. That medicine made me vomit a lot and within days I quit taking it, because without knowing I had the condition, I felt it was worth the risk to end the medication. Frankly, it was all too much. I couldn't vomit anything more out of my body. I couldn't keep food down. I felt terrible physically and emotionally. I had tested negative for HIV and was told until the 10-year mark, I wasn't home free. It could show up one day. When I reached that anniversary date, I cannot fully express the added relief in knowing I was finally free of that concern shedding one more aspect of this rape aftermath. It was no small thing for my spirit.

I had reluctantly gone out that night at my sister's urging to a birthday party with a group she and her boyfriend knew after originally planning to stay home and read. Toward the end of the evening, one guy in this bigger circle of kids I understood to all be friends wanted everyone to go to one person's house. I was 21 and did not have a sordid drinking history. I had had two wine coolers over the course of four hours and here's what's interesting about my choice. I was not lightheaded or feeling tipsy, but in my inexperience with this kind of scene my choice was made out of hyper-responsibility. I understood 'don't drink and drive' and then and now take it seriously, but this was before widespread designated driver initiatives. One guy in the group said this kid I had only just met had not been drinking at all and he could drive. He'd been a nice guy, clean cut, a well-known athlete, and seemed friendly with people around there. We were all going just a few blocks together in several cars, so it didn't seem like a concern. Everything seemed on the up and up. In fact, it seemed like the mature decision. My hyper-responsibility did me in that night. I trusted his human decency.

I could regret sharing some of this information if I wasn't solid in my view that human dignity is our vital landing place on this topic. I was a crystal clear snapshot of who this was 'not supposed to' happen to with my background, habits, and responsible nature and, still, it did. My scenario is a good illustration of why attempts to shame women for what they wear, drink, or their sexual past after rape make no difference. It's distracting, compounds pain in useless ways, and takes focus away from where it belongs on the perpetrator.

I know the attack was not my fault. My allowing him to drive my car does not excuse his behavior and looking for more and more ways for women to take responsibility for poor male behavior will never solve this human problem. We do men an injustice when we allow it.

One of the severest strikes to my self-worth was when he finally drove himself home and pulled in his own driveway between 5:30-6:00 in the morning. He said before he'd get out of the car, he wanted me to give him my phone number. I had not said a word the rest of the night or on the ride back to his house, as I was petrified. I silently robotically wrote down my phone number on a scrap of paper and he took it. What would he do if I didn't give it to him? I didn't feel like I had a choice if I wanted to get back to my life. The shame and confusion mixed with awareness it was the only decision for my sense of safety so he'd 'allow' me to leave messed with me for years. It was a difficult process of overcoming to reach a place of self-forgiveness for that one action alone. It still sparks emotion now as I write about it, because I have such compassion for the young woman in that car. I know now, in retrospect, that phone number expectation was his way of making himself believe what he did was ok, even desirable. He could tell himself that I wanted what he did to me, whatever that was, and his ego and sense of entitlement could remain intact. In his mind, he had evidence. The pounding of the trauma was already in play for me.

I didn't go back to the community where it happened for many years. I couldn't bring myself to do it. I thought it would feel like I was drowning myself and I wasn't up for flailing around in that water. It didn't seem necessary.

I could only call what happened an attack and an assault for a long time, as well. I couldn't bring myself to call it sexual assault or rape. The shame was too intense. We understand no one deserves to be assaulted or attacked, so using those two words was simpler, cleaner, and a wash of shame didn't drench me, because of the sexual responsibility we place on woman as a society.

As time went on and I was able to work my way through the different pieces of it all, I began to realize calling anything about it sex was humiliating and embarrassing. It didn't feel true. When I used the word sex, it felt like I was inviting people into my intimate life. It was so intensely personal. Calling it rape? It took a long time to own that as what it was - rape. I was socialized as and rewarded for being a conscientious, caring kid and rape was a serious declaration and disconnect from how I'd been identified to myself as a teenager and eventually young adult. I couldn't make it all fit together.

I had a clear, articulate voice, but was still trying to learn how to own it without apologizing for its strength, because I was already trying to balance the split in how employers wanted me to be and how I knew I was as me. Since I didn't enjoy pretending and playing games, I found it all frustrating and difficult.

For a long time, allowing myself to call it rape equated to putting a spotlight on my demand to be seen by those around me in college and starting my career. Those were places the messages I was receiving made it clear the preference was for women who were simple, pleasant, didn't make a fuss, energetic, pleasing, youthful, uncomplicated, pretty, sharp, and tough in a cute pat-me-on-the-head way. But, I had my own assertive voice that did not always fit the mold. I worked to reconcile that for years, so I could stay true to myself. Having been sexually assaulted made my hyper-focus in finding the balance more pronounced and urgent to me, so I could progress in attempting to make sense of the world around me.

RAPE RAVAGES SELF-ESTEEM

Rape left me doubting my self-worth. It's another situation that calls into question the assumed meaning of every single word to rethink in this book. I saved rape for last, because it's weighty and perceived to be one of the more horrifying experiences to endure and it is. It's a silent epidemic so many people share in, but don't talk about despite the fact it impacts how we relate to the world around us.

I walk through my experience of rape to share what is seared into my memory as my self-worth was getting pummeled by what felt like a brutalizing hostile invasion and its aftermath. From the attack itself to my perspective on the bigger picture afterward, it's rippled through my life. Many decisions I've made have been as a result of the sexual assault. That includes choices in who to and not to be around making up good chunks of our human experience. It also impacts something as mundane as changing travel routes, so I'm not known by name in gas stations which

I've done several times over the years. I've often consciously made it a point to leave my workplaces at different times each week or not park my car in the same place over and over to attempt to make my patterns harder to pin down. It's so well-engrained, I don't even consider the fact I pay attention to stair wells, dark corners, elevators, dark rooms and darkness, in general, or even underneath my car when I approach it in public parking to make sure I see no human threat. I quickly look in the backseat of my car each time I get in and I'm silently annoyed getting into vehicles with dark windows, because I can't see inside as easily. I'm always touched when a man steps out of an elevator if he realizes we'll be alone nodding at me with a kind smile without us even exchanging words. He understands. This is a very short partial list of only a few ways being sexually assaulted, as well as being a woman, has impacted my life.

It's primarily below the surface and part of my routine now, but that it's part of me means it's an accepted fear I'm so used to living with I no longer consider it abnormal to have to do it. Does that mean I live in subconscious fear of men? How can it not if I'm regularly adjusting behavior knowing no one will feel for me if I'm attacked or hurt and didn't take proper precautions as if the behavior of others is my responsibility? How can that not set up women for falls in multiple ways in their lives? My behavior is my responsibility and the behavior of others is their responsibility. I'm embarrassed to even type much of this paragraph as I like to consider myself strong able to stand on my own two feet. But, what I share begs the legitimate question of whether I've been culturally conditioned to fear men through actual violating behavior at the hands of a few. I believe all of us must address this question together to ever hope to solve it in expanding our cultural consciousness.

How can this kind of quiet fear of being physically overpowered and hurt again not impact how you make other decisions in your life? I've wanted to take walks in my own very safe neighborhood at night and found myself debating whether I was up to dealing with the possibility of bumping into some problem person on my path. Do I bother walking knowing I'll be on automatic high alert? Am I in the mood to feel anxious?

There's no certain script for these ordeals, but as I walked step by step through each moment in my healing process over the years I knew my dignity and self-pride had been impacted in multiple ways. How does one emerge fully healed and intact after painful ordeals is the question I found myself attempting to answer over and over again even years after having been raped.

A THINKING WOMAN & RAPE AFTERMATH

We know in the broader cultural conversation shaken loose with the #MeToo movement countless people relate to the terror of this kind of scene having been through it themselves with the distinctions of their own very personal experiences. No matter how much you've worked through this invasion, it has a way of coloring life differently.

Rape is a trip to hell and I had to decide if I'd come back. Plus, if I did come back from that, I didn't know how that would look. I didn't have an adequate answer. After a few months of grappling, trying to face it and decide who I was now after this invasion, I shut it down with no certain answers. Occasionally, I'd mention it with a highly trusted friend or workmate in hope the sharing would reduce the shame of living in silence about the unjust ordeal as if I was detoxing by reaching out for help to get poison out of my body. I had to get on with my life for now. I was 21 when this happened, learning to define myself. My self definition? I didn't know how to see myself with this pain and damage forced on me. I was not a promiscuous person which added a dimension to my processing the entire ordeal. Does this kind of damaging behavior bounce off of us or seep into our pores, settle in our souls, and make us different? It was a question I was now trying to answer for myself.

I asked myself if my life could be better after rape. I didn't have an answer. It took years to realize how that definition decision was purely, utterly mine. You owe no one an explanation or justification for your self-definition. It's your birthright. You are you without apology. But, unfortunately after rape, I found myself apologizing to myself and others about my pain. At times, I found others taking it so hard, I was tasked with holding them up about my having been raped. I didn't expect that which turned into useful learning about the fragility in all of us.

That said I don't believe some men who sexually assault women believe they've done it. That seems to be what entitlement is all about and is worthy of note. I base my view, in part, on my own experience as is evident. It means I'm less than convinced we're reaching each other in these broader cultural conversations and that has to change somehow.

I didn't drink at all in high school except for trying some raspberry-colored mixed drink to see what it tasted like at my sister's wedding at 15 because it looked pretty. This is not the stuff of riveting books. I tried my very first beer around the kitchen table at a girlfriend's house on her family farm with her, me, and another close friend watching the effects it had on me in real time while lovingly policing my safety. It was done in such a trusting, caring environment I chuckle now thinking about it, because of the sense of responsibility my friends had for me. One went on to become a nurse and the other one went into security. It was pretty much the ideal combination to insure my safety that night during the second half of my freshman year in college when I was 18.

My siblings displayed empathy in their words and actions

which I'm grateful for to this day - all five of them. People react differently. For example, my brother, Mark, and his wife gave me a bouquet of flowers and kind words. My sister, Mary Zita, among many other things some of which I've mentioned, had my car detailed to eliminate memory triggers. Plus, for Christmas that year she gave me a basket full of car accessories to redecorate it in the spirit of building new memories. My little sister heard about what happened shortly after we returned from the hospital emergency room. I went up to my dusty blue as we called it childhood bedroom and collapsed for hard won sleep feeling world weary. Michelle walked in the front door, exchanged words with my parents, and ran upstairs into my room hurling herself on my bed clutching at me wailing that she was so very sorry about what I had been put through all night.

I remember Mary Zita taking me to my attorney brother's house a couple days after my return from the emergency room. I was feeling shattered knowing I had to finish my fall semester as a university Senior with only weeks to go. My older brother, Mick, told me I had 10 days from the incident to file sexual assault charges and one year to file battery charges if the guy ever contacted me again. I was already a few days into that ticking clock situation at this point. I was in shock feeling embarrassed, ashamed, confused, afraid, and in utter disbelief at the cruelty of this person. I mean I handed him my phone number, so did I really have a leg to stand on if he actually called the number? I was nowhere near having a big picture view of the situation yet. Making the decision to press charges for rape was too much to process at that time because my focus was my pain and getting well, trying to get back to my life, and find a way to cope with fear while addressing the trauma.

I counted off the days of that year knowing I, at least, had the battery charge response in my favor if he ever tried to contact me again which did give me some strength and a tiny sense of safety.

I grappled with my responsibility to others at the time in my desire to press charges, but feared doing it. I felt so badly for not doing it. I'm not one to shrink from that kind of responsibility to others. Starting out in my career, though, I worried it would taint my possibility for employment. Even though we know it's not supposed to, that's not necessarily the reality. I worried about my name getting attached to the idea and without a stronger self-definition at that age, I feared that would be how I was defined. Plus, I was hurting and when talking to Mary Zita about it all, her words helped me decide. She said, "Maria, you do, at this time, what helps your own healing." With so few days to decide and a desire to stay on track in college coursework, I chose my own healing. I feared justice might be elusive and my reputation, which was stellar, would be smeared and I'd never overcome it in my career. It was 1990-91 and I'm glad to say a different time. Today it would be different. At least I hope it would be different.

I'M WORTH MORE THAN RAPE

I hate owning rape as mine. My rape? There's strong philosophy on this as an act of strength, but I don't want it. I didn't want it and I don't claim it. I was brutalized. I don't want to own that. That's on the rapist. He owns it and if he doesn't? It'll sit there until every story told by every survivor shedding shame breaks through and we collectively see humanity in every human being. We don't own any other crime. Felonies? Is it my criminal damage to property?

Why is it we take possession of rape, but can't own having been a victim for even a few months after brutality when we desperately need the softness and care? We quickly learn that if we do allow ourselves to be called a victim, we risk our own reputation as stable, strong, and productive members of society. Nobody seems to respect a victim. A victim is often pitied, at best, which involves a thread of arrogance not useful to their healing and can actually work against it. Victim-blamers are bullies.

What I do own is my story. There's power and beauty in my awareness of my worth shining in that knowledge. But, I don't ever refer to the rape as my rape. I never will.

Counseling wasn't the automatic go to in my realm at that time. I didn't know where to put this trauma. I put some of it in exercise. I put some of it in career. I read constantly. I did slide into the eating disordered behavior as I talk more directly about in the earlier chapters called Anger and Regret and it took me a couple years after the sexual assault to find an adequate solution. I seized as many opportunities as I could to spend time in nature. I put some of the trauma residue into music by building a library of strong female singer-songwriters channeling anger there. I perfected my ability to articulate my vision of a better world through volunteer and professional work, specifically, with a focus on helping people find and use their voice. Over the years, it's contributed greatly to my increased sensitivity to injustice, bullying, and entitlement. Plus, I learned on some level through the ordeal that being a woman was a safety liability.

I apologized to myself for a period of time for not being a man to avoid the vulnerability of my femininity. I locked the door on the trauma. About ten years later as the final days of my HIV concerns dissolved away, all of the memories rushed back in a kind of torrential rain storm of tears and shuddering silent cries on the basement floor of my townhouse alone where nobody could see trying to understand why I couldn't shed it all through sheer will.

I learned people can't give you what they don't have for themselves. Most people can't even attempt to hold your grief with you, because they often can't or are barely able to hold their own. It's tough for many people to dig into life at a deeper level than what's on the surface.

Victim-blaming is a distancing tactic. No one finds comfort for their day to day lives in the idea of indiscriminate crime. It's chaos. Safety is not supposed to be ambiguous for us to feel secure as human beings. But, I've learned people only think they're safe and secure. It's a tidy story we tell ourselves subconsciously to be able to function in the world. Without it, so many of us would crumble in a blob of fear and insecurity unless we learn there's power in ambiguity and randomness that can strengthen us with less to rely on at any given second. My process of overcoming this pain was letting it sink in that we must rely on ourselves for self-worth while taking no other human experience for granted around us. Our ability to be vulnerable puts us at risk, but is also a precious gift to ourselves and others when it's kindly regarded and delicately held.

Sex and rape are not the same thing and this distinction was an important one in my reclaiming self-worth. If someone forces an object down your throat such as a cucumber, are you eating? Of course not. The stark visual that idea conjures is intentional. Rape is called a sex crime. Why do we accept that connection?

Sex and rape are not the same thing. If someone forces an object down your throat such as a cucumber, are you eating? Of course not. Rape is called a sex crime. Why do we accept that connection?

We live in a culture that makes victims, and very often that's women, responsible for sexual assault which sabotages self-value because you cannot possibly control the decisions and actions of other people. There's a fundamental intellectual disconnect in the victim-blaming mindset. Growing up, kids snicker with friends to make sense of what they're told are adult topics. I remember hearing 'You can't rape the willing' in the hallways said out of childish ignorance in an attempt at humor. The kids saying it didn't fully understand the implication of their words. Neither did I. We were junior high and high school kids and the topic was taboo. When you hear someone so fearful of it and its aftermath say, "I'd rather be dead than raped." a young girl adds rape to the list of ideas that are her responsibility to avoid if she wants to stay alive. Plus, girls are often taught that sex is always their responsibility however it happened. We are taught to be gatekeepers of sexual behavior through clothing choices, our personality, physicality, and even geographic location at any given time. It's changing, but is not widespread enough to tip the balance.

On the flip side, do boys then internalize the message they should not perpetrate it? Not being a boy, I don't know. I have never heard a guy say he worked at growing into a man who would not rape, learning the signs, checking his behavior, policing behavior of other boys and men, and being careful where he went to avoid becoming a rapist. It sounds outrageous. I certainly don't want to think that of any male I know. But, if a man can blame a woman at the outset for all of the reasons I've stated above and also never believe he has a responsibility to learn not to rape, where is he in the scenario? It's as if he gets to vanish in how we have set this up culturally and yet he is often the culprit. How does that work and why is this so easy to overlook? Some humility in all of us has benefits.

When you tell someone you've been raped, you learn about them. You can find yourself soothing them about your experience which is confusing and draining to self-worth. People ask what you were wearing, what time, and where you were to decide whether or not you 'deserved' it. A few look at you with empathy, but resignation about gender saying, "MEN!" and that response might be the saddest I heard as I worked through my own untangling of rape from gender over the years. You can't write off an entire gender because some don't use their power for good.

You're quizzed about specifics, so people can decide how to distance themselves from your pain and circumstances which can add a few more cracks to your self-worth. They want to avoid your path as if you chose it willingly. It's another subtle form of victim-blaming. The question asker teaches themselves how to avoid rape when you're asking for a listening ear not offering a workshop on 'How To Avert Rape 101.' It adds a layer to the feeling of being sidelined in life for a while. There are many ways rape and its aftermath wreck self-worth.

STAY TUNED FOR RAPE AFTER THIS

Rape as mindless, even titillating entertainment doesn't support the rebuilding of self-worth after you've been attacked. Some people think they're sensitive to rape, but watch it over and over in entertainment. We often hear about how we're desensitized to things we're exposed to a lot. For example, I can be bothered by the fact my mail needs sorting, but after a while get used to setting it aside, finding it easier and easier to overlook. That only changes if I stay aware and present which is not easy to do all the time.

So many people have been raped and don't talk about trauma they carry, a disconnect for a lot of survivors is in having to navigate a world that doesn't take it seriously enough without realizing just how many of us there actually are. When you're too afraid to share the trauma understanding from what you've witnessed culturally that you won't be believed or embraced and the culture around you, in general, reflects an attitude that your dignity isn't valued, a tragic inner crumbling starts to take place in silent suffering. It's awful. There is a social shift taking place slowly, but we're only at the very beginning stages of change.

Sexual assault aftermath is usually missing in entertainment, which is disappointing, because if rape is going to be used to move along a plot line, aftermath provides an opportunity to employ empathy or learn to build some. This impacts self-worth. Representation of that aftermath can cause its own kind of difficulty if it's not handled responsibly, but without aftermath and witnessing the emotional rocky trek back to health, we get shock value and episodic drama. But, break for a commercial and it's over. I am well aware dwelling on emotional aftermath of this brutality doesn't necessarily help movie pacing, but the fact the path after rape is not something we see enough in mainstream media programming is relevant to self-worth. Rape is not mindless entertainment.

Rape is not mindless entertainment.

I remember watching a rape scene so painful to view I couldn't even get through it, because I knew what it felt like for me. I probably could have watched it, if I hadn't experienced it which might have left me wondering about it. I was sitting in my living room watching a movie called Monster starring Charlize Theron, enough of a reason to watch any movie her work is so wonderful and powerful and, often, important to the collective cultural conversation. I remember the date, March 17th, 2004. That's how impactful the moment was for me.

I was several months pregnant with my first child at the time. I sat in shuddering tears watching the main character get attacked at a pick up truck. Eventually, I turned it off. I was in pain watching it. This was almost 15 years after having been raped to share how the memory of this violation rippled through my own life.

I was in pain for myself knowing what that kind of fear feels like. I was in pain for the baby girl I was carrying wondering what life had in store for her wanting to protect her from harm. I was in pain for the world knowing rape doesn't have to happen and that each human being is worth so much more than that. I was in pain for the person who dares rape another thinking it is whatever answer they're after in the moment.

I'd never fallen apart before watching a movie rape scene, but then again I try to avoid them or avert my eyes, because I can feel that pain from a distance. Without a solution to end these crimes, how many people numb themselves or are re-traumatized for the sake of keeping peace? They don't make a big deal out of what they went through, don't reveal it afraid they'll be hurt again through judgment, being dismissed, ostracized, or, ultimately, re-victimized. I walked through all of that at different times. It's messed up and part of culture. Rape blatantly and insidiously impacts self-esteem.

Rape blatantly and insidiously impacts self-esteem.

You go through life after this kind of traumatic experience and you learn to stand up again. At the same time, you find yourself chipped at in a 1000 ways from music references and off-the-hook celebrities, to rape kits languishing due to expense or lack of knowledge and training to process, which equates to trivializing its impact and importance to the health and well-being of our society. Significant strides are being made in this regard, but there's a long way to go. It adds up to verbal and non-verbal indications this is not one of the significant crimes.

In fact, the message can become the idea you might be to blame for your own situation. The cultural message when rape crimes are not taken seriously can play in a way that indicates what you say you went through is so much trouble, we don't even want to bother dealing with it.

When casual or formal sports banter allows use of the word rape to describe how one team takes advantage of another team, it disrespects survivors. Survivors are not a sport to be conquered. We're human beings. You hear people using the word as a black and white certainty in sports references. Yet, you know from watching media reports, the chance of anyone believing the rape you went through for real is grey, at very best. We trust the truth of the word rape only when points are at stake? It's outrageous.

WHY IS RAPE CALLED A SEX CRIME?

Why isn't rape referred to as a penetration, physical invasion, or body violation crime? It's not sex. Some might get clinical and say that's wrong, but my respectful gynecologist does not have sex with me every time I, willingly, get an exam just because focus is on that region of the body. Some might sensibly point out that I made the appointment, so I chose to go to the office. Yes, but I didn't ask for the probe. He decided that is what was necessary for my desired health outcome. Physical presence anywhere does not mean putting something in the vagina is imminent and an entitlement.

If I'm in my car and someone else decides the outcome will be a penetration of my body in a way we call sexual assault, why does the perpetrator's perspective have precedence over my perspective as a survivor of that moment. It confuses the issue and adds to the entire big picture problem that leads to victim blaming. If we called gynecological exams sex exams, it'd be creepy, obscene, and inaccurate.

If we called gynecological exams sex exams, it'd be creepy, obscene, and inaccurate.

Rape is not a sex crime. Sex involves consent. When there is no consent, it is no longer having sex. It is now a type of criminal damage case. My hunch is more people would report the crime if we looked at this one idea differently. Remove the word sex from descriptions of these crimes. Too often we don't even take on the actual happenings of the crime, because we get stuck on consent as if it was even on the table all because the word sex is involved. As long as anyone is able to argue consent, survivors won't see the kind of validation sought in the search for justice.

Years ago, a college psychology professor friend mentioned giving surveys at the beginning of the semester asking students how many sex partners they've had as part of coursework preparations. My immediate response was does rape count? She was taken aback and horrified at the idea, ultimately, updating wording in the survey. It's a point worth making and sits out there as a cultural contradiction. The message to survivors in social dialogue is confusing, at best.

Plenty of people think of the word sex and immediately jump to positive adjectives or moral ones which doesn't keep responsibility where it belongs - on the person committing the violation. When you use sex as a primary word to describe a crime, it's not surprising to hear people attempt to downplay its seriousness and even believe you wanted it to happen or enjoyed it when it did. Or, find themselves in some warped way insulted you were chosen in a social scene and they weren't which is full of all kinds of head-scratching confusion. I have run into this over the years and don't know what to make of it except to say we will do ourselves so many favors when women learn that being contentedly, happily alone is so much better than accepting so very little from another human being. Sexual harassment, sexual assault, and rape are no compliment and not a competition.

Sexual assault and rape are no compliment and not a competition.

A crime is a crime is a crime. We understand crime is a bad thing. We understand rape is a bad thing. Sex is not a word that works that way and it needs to be eliminated when describing rape. As citizens, we can understand the seeming connections and grapple with how sex and rape seem to mix together in certain ways at times. However, at an official level it makes sense to require more from our growth, learning, and awareness upping the certainty that rape and sex are not equitable and won't be lumped into the same idea in our use of legal verbiage.

They're wound together and, yet, not connected at all like a hair braid which might make what I suggest seem impossible. But, consider this. We've increasingly refused to accept the idea in this culture that no means anything except no. That hasn't always been the case and has been no easy change. It's taken years for that to take hold and now we know no matter what a scene looks or feels like, when someone says no to another person's body against their own, it means no.

The haziness of the line between sex and rape added a dimension to my own victimization wondering if I'd caused my own predicament, because it's all so tough to work through in following days and months. I did not cause it. It was not my fault. Without the word sex attached to the crime, I could've more easily acted on it as a crime, not something to be upset with myself for because I didn't see it coming and didn't protect myself adequately enough. Continuing to send a cultural message that woman are responsible for the behavior of people who mistreat them will not help us build positive loving mutually respectful relationships en masse until we champion a major shift on this one point alone. I could have more easily jumped to the fact it did not diminish my value as a woman if I hadn't been staring at the baggage sex brings with it in this culture as a wide-eyed 21-year-old principled female. That took longer than it needed to, as a result. Learning how to stand up again after a trauma and own your perspective is a path back to self-worth. All of this awareness has rebuilt my self-worth over the years stronger than before one day at a time

WHO WE CHOOSE TO BE

In conversations, I've asked men if they were to see a woman walking down the street naked, what's their first instinct? Is it to offer help or decide whether or not her body turns him on? I'm not asking what he acts on. I'm asking what his first thought is. Is it to be of service or the opposite? I don't know the answer. I'd guess it varies. Some women get angry with this idea as a way to make objectification, power, control, and sex about clothing. But, it's not that at all. My hunch is if we want men to join the discussion, we have to allow them space to consider and discuss their own instincts, socialization, views, and experiences without immediately slamming their responses. Is their starting point a humble service-minded one or one of entitlement?

This question above points to the consideration women receive in even the most vulnerable circumstances. The answer a person comes to for themselves in this question is worthy of personal investigation. Is a woman safe anywhere and in any circumstances, really? It's a startling idea. I say this knowing many wonderful, sensitive, thoughtful men.

It's common for people to immediately shut down clothing coverage and fit as not a factor in rape. I agree. It's not. However, the missing follow up question each time I hear this point made is: Has anyone talked about this idea to men who objectify and perpetrate the crimes? Do they know they're not connected?

We can sit in judgment and awareness of disconnects, but we have to involve men who make decisions to objectify or abuse, assault, or rape for whatever reasons they do. Do they realize those assumed clothing cues are not about the women sending messages, but about their own decision-making processes? How can we require a man change behavior, but not ask this question? If we don't allow the question, we risk building a worse problem of fostering more shame and suppression in men than already exists attempting to find common ground on these topics. Effective collective preserving and building of self-worth impacts all of us.

If you can't prove sexual assault or rape with enough credible witnesses, it's not real. I think that's the toughest aspect of this dialogue. When people take or steal something from us, how often do they do it with a crowd of witnesses? Not often. You commonly see people talk past each other on social media in the very idea. But, what if it's a crime primarily committed in privacy? How do we address that as a country? This adds a layer in handing females responsibility for male behavior given that the vast majority of sexual assaults involves female victims. How can self-worth survive that kind of heavy-duty expectation?

I understand the legitimate fear of its opposite with men at the mercy of an unethical woman out to get them, but that's rare and women live with their fear, in most situations, every day and have for eons. What's the remedy? Women cannot be held responsible or hold themselves responsible for policing male behavior. If you're roughed up in an alley where no one sees it happen, what's the chance you'll be believed if you only have your story and no witnesses. Wouldn't you expect to be believed when you go to authorities? Or, would you tell yourself you're out of luck because you didn't make sure it happened in front of others? Somewhere in the middle of all of this there has to be a solution.

I've walked you through the experience of unexpectedly having my self-worth smashed, as well as my walk back to center through a few pieces of my process that include feeling the feelings and accepting a new reality, plus owning my perspective and trusting I have something to say in what can help spark change. Each person's experience is very different and each path will be, as well. But, it's useful to see some of the many layers in trying to re-ground yourself after such a significant trauma.

Sexual assault is an emotionally exhausting topic. It's hard. It's yucky. It's not empowering to think about intimate violations day after day. It can feel like you're getting dragged down by the enormity of the issue. Plus, it can start to seep into you when that frustration, anger, and feeling of futility need a place to go. I know I'm not defined by those events I experienced in the past, but it's still not easy to keep it from piercing me a little too deeply once in a while challenging my sense of self even all these years later.

There are cultural contradictions that compound the difficulty in a person's healing after rape and each can impact self-worth. Ultimately, rape was the lesson for me that I won't be cornered again. I'll always have my own back and, if feeling dangerously unsafe, I'll fight back because that's what having self-worth means to me in my particular life.

Rethink Challenge: Your challenge is to see worth as within your control. Can you see the distinction between an external value of worth and an internal view of your worth? Your view of your worth is where you start to build your external reality. You have value, just because you are here. Your worth is yours to determine, no one else's. You can decide that human dignity is non-negotiable starting with your own.

TAKE MY WORD FOR IT

Each journey is personal, but we impact each other. The words we think and say are a huge part of it. As adults, rethinking how we experience and apply terminology we were taught as kids has value in approaching our mature years in a more conscious, connected way.

I'm in a wonderful place in my life. I am peaceful, content, and happy. I love who my kids are as people. They have caring hearts and see the world with kind eyes. I've had a fascinating stellar career that continues to evolve and I enjoy the journey immensely. The people I choose to surround myself with are special, loving, fun, giving, creative people who see the best in each other and want to celebrate and support each other's pursuit of their best selves. What more could I ask for? Little, if anything.

Here are few final thoughts to help you stay centered and focused on what matters working through adversities in life and in words we use to describe them. This list can help you in your own healing.

When I lose track of myself and fall off-center, I tether myself to these ideas below and work my way back to center again in peace and contentment.

We hear the ideas of exercise, good nutrition, meditation, and having good people around us being good medicine when overcoming adversity, but there are other more basic and less discussed ideas I've found to be useful in my own journey.

1- Slow down - Just stop. Take a deep breath. Give that anxiousness that can build up a chance to dissipate. Do it again and again till it sticks. Yeah, it feels weird for a while.

2- Make deliberate choices. When you know why you make decisions, there are fewer regrets to fuel discontent. It's not about making perfect choices to get straight A's on the report card of life. It's about understanding yourself better.

3- Shed perfectionism. Strive for personal excellence, not perfectionism. You can be mellow on one topic and perfectionistic on another, so pay close attention. You might catch remnants you didn't think much about before. Clean out that contaminated thinking.

4- Let sadness move through you. Fight the urge to pretend it's not there when it takes you. Just be with it. It gives you something authentic to measure moments of joy against helping keep life balanced and in perspective.

5- Quit performing for people. Leave the performing where it belongs; the stage. You don't have to entertain people for the right ones to want to be around you. When you externalize your value that way, you invite emptiness and discontentment to set in.

6- Shun comparisons. Don't waste your life comparing it to everyone else. It's shallow and useless. There are so many major and minor factors that put people where they are - some within their control and some entirely out of their control. Sometimes what looks like success is a tenuous cover for a lot of unhappiness. Sometimes the happiest people keep life simplest and expenses lowest. There are so many twists and turns and life is known to turn on a dime.

Don't buy in 100% to the idea we're each in control of everything that happens in our lives. There's plenty we do control, but much we don't. Just ask a woman who did everything 'right' having a baby and faced something unforeseen. That was a huge wake up call for me, personally, and little talked about in my sphere. My body ran with pregnancy. I had less control than I assumed I would going in as I enthusiastically followed the pregnancy 'rulebook.' It was its own deal, so how could I compare it to anyone else?

7- Do what you love to do. Even if it's not your regular job, make time for something you love to do in your free time. It will fuel you and give you something to think about that feeds your soul. Who knows? With time, maybe that will become your career if it didn't start out that way. Life has a funny way of working out differently than we planned.

8- Get fresh air. Walk, ride a bike, go outside and say hi to a neighbor, make weekend trekking to various farmers markets your thing maybe (sharing one of my things). Just go and do something where you can hear a few birds, feel a little vitamin D pick me up from the sun on your shoulders, hear a breeze move through the leaves of a tree, and be around some life forms that aren't just you. I'm not talking crowds. I'm talking about finding just a smidge of vibrancy to appreciate. Sometimes, the best medicine has no words.

9- Make a list of you. Make a list of everything you have accomplished and give yourself permission to feel amazed by yourself once in a while. It doesn't have to be grand resume ready accomplishments. It could be something as simple as… You know what? I take great care of my garden and it's a really cool space. A periodic self-assessment check in is good for the soul. It reminds us we are actually getting somewhere.

One of my more meaningful moments in recent years came when I was fighting to stand up again after divorce and an old friend and colleague offered to write me a professional letter of recommendation having not expected anything of him. I'd lost sight of the fact I mattered until I read that letter. It gave me strength to know something I did impacted someone else in a useful, helpful way. It helped me build new strength. It's easy to lose sight of that when you're deeply hurting. After that, I thought it'd be a good healing tool for people in my situation in the future. Request a letter of recommendation to help you stand up again. It's kind, constructive, and forward-focused, yet using the past to build a bright new future. Words can hurt or heal us and those words, for me, were healing.

10- Require it of yourself to stay honest with you. Life does not have to be complicated. When a person tries to convince someone life is messy and complicated, they're often giving themselves permission to lie to you. It doesn't have to be that way. Life can be simple, calm, pleasant, and kind.

11- Eliminate toxic people from your life. People who are caustic, rude, selfish, manipulatively nice, insensitive, thoughtlessly cruel, dehumanizing, shallow, and dismissive all qualify for removal from circles of trust in my book.

Move your life in the direction of people committed to living authentically, capable of being vulnerable, willing to express their care for you and others, willing to receive the care you give, and who want to foster a sense of belonging with you because they love you for who you are and vice versa. Words matter.

12- Work on your self-soothing skills. What you say to yourself and how you think of the words you use matter.

You're awesome just because you're here. You're right where

you're supposed to be. You have extraordinary things to offer and you've impacted people's lives in wonderful ways. You're loved and cared about and appreciated for your unique gifts. You matter and your heart is precious.

Ok, now go say this last one to yourself in the mirror until you believe it at the core of your being, because you really are awesome.

Peace to you, my friend.

Love,
Maria

.

Printed in the United States
By Bookmasters